THE UNIVERSITY AS
RES PUBLICA

Higher education governance, student participation and the university as a site of citizenship

Sjur Bergan (editor)

Council of Europe Publishing

Council of Europe Publishing
F-67075 Strasbourg Cedex

ISBN 92-871-5515-1
© Council of Europe, November 2004
Printed at the Council of Europe

Contents

Preface

The book you are about to read explores various aspects of the role of the university as a site of democratic citizenship, ranging from student participation in higher education governance to the higher education institution as an actor in democratic society. The articles outline how teaching and practice within the university have an impact on the development and maintenance of democratic culture in the larger society, and they give a practical example through the description of the development of a student charter in one of the Council of Europe's newer member states, Moldova.

This book underlines the importance and contribution of education and higher education to the overall political objectives of the Council of Europe: democracy, human rights and the rule of law. Education is in many ways the vital element that will ensure that these objectives are essential practices of modern European society rather than lofty ideals admired at a distance. However democratic its institutional and legal framework, no society can be truly democratic except through practice, and democratic practice is fostered through education for democratic citizenship.

This is why the Council of Europe has declared 2005 to be the European Year of Citizenship through Education, and the present book is one of the contributions of our higher education sector to the Year. The book draws on a number of activities that the Council of Europe has already carried out in this area and lays the groundwork to this Year for all parts of the education sector.

I would like to take this opportunity to thank the Norwegian Ministry of Education, Research and Church Affairs for its consent to include two articles that were originally a Council of Europe contribution to a seminar on Student Participation in Higher Education Governance organised in Oslo in June 2003. I would also like to thank our United States and European partners for their co-operation in the pilot project on the University as Site of Citizenship and the group of students and teachers at the Ion Creangă State Pedagogical University in Chişinău, who elaborated a student charter within the Council of Europe project on Education for Democratic Citizenship.

I would also like to thank the authors of the different articles for this book, and, not least, I would like to thank the two immediate past chairs of the Council's Steering Committee for Higher Education and Research (CD-ESR) – Krzysztof Ostrowski and Per Nyborg – as well as the current chair – Věra Šťastná – for their continuing commitment to higher education in Europe based on the values of the Council of Europe. The articles in this book arise from activities carried out under their chairmanship of the CD-ESR.

Gabriele Mazza
Director of School, Out-of-School and Higher Education
Council of Europe

A word from the editor

Sjur Bergan

The image of the university as an ivory tower seems to be a universal one. Like many images it may hold a grain of truth but, like most stereotypes, it is not free of misconceptions. The grain of truth stems from a basic facet of academic life: academic learning and research aim to discover and transmit the fundamental elements of human existence as well as the human-made and natural world. This requires adequate distance from the pressures of daily life, the daily social, political, cultural and economic agenda and daily headlines. This is even more important in the age of the sound bite, where planning horizons rarely seem to go beyond the short term and public attention spans seem to shrink. In this sense, the university is of this world, but only partly in it.

Yet, higher education institutions cannot lead an existence totally divorced from the societies of which they are a part. University autonomy is an important part of the heritage of European universities, but autonomy cannot mean total isolation from the larger society. If the university had sought to be not only autonomous but self-sufficient, it would have ceased to be relevant to society, and it is very doubtful whether the university would have survived as one of the most time-honoured institutions of European society, along with church and parliament. The heritage of European universities is precisely the story of how universities have changed their form, their methodology and their focus to preserve their core mission: that of being useful to society while maintaining sufficient distance from the agenda of the day to offer the kind of service that society needs so badly and that no other institution can provide: the long-term development of the fundamental competences and values without which our societies can neither develop nor survive.[1]

Higher education institutions, then, are key elements of modern societies, and in more ways than one. The present book focuses on one of these ways, namely the development and maintenance of the democratic culture without which democratic institutions cannot work and democratic laws will remain a dead letter.

In this sense, education is particularly important to the main concerns of the Council of Europe – democracy, human rights and the rule of law – and all the articles in the present work originate in Council of Europe activities addressing the role of higher education in the larger society of which it is a part.

In the first article, I seek to place the issue of student participation in the wider context of the university as an actor in democratic society and as an essential partner in developing democratic culture. This role is underlined

---

[1] See Nuria Sanz and Sjur Bergan (eds): *The Heritage of European Universities,* Strasbourg: Council of Europe Publishing, 2002.

through the shift from considering the university as a *teaching* institution to considering it as a *learning* institution. Democratic practice can certainly be studied, and it deserves to be, but it cannot be learned from books and in auditoriums alone. Democratic practice can be internalised only by actually practising it and participating in it. Therefore, teaching and studying democratic governance in theoretical terms at higher education level is of limited value unless institutions also reflect democratic practice and values in their internal life, in particular in their governance structures.

Nevertheless, higher education institutions are not student run, as they most likely would have been if the principle of "one person, one vote" had applied to institutional governance. Rather, higher education governance is a balance between two different sets of principles: that of equal representation according to numbers, and that of representation according to an individual's stake in the institution and their competence with regard to the institution's main mission.

While the principle of student participation in higher education governance is well established in Europe, practice varies somewhat from country to country and from one level of governance to another. More importantly, however, it seems increasingly difficult to motivate students to participate in and contribute to higher education governance.

The issues raised in the first article are explored in further detail in the following two articles. The second article, like the first one, was presented at the follow-up Bologna seminar on Student Participation in Higher Education Governance organised in Oslo on 12-14 June 2003 by the Norwegian Ministry of Education,[2] and we are grateful to the ministry for its permission to use the articles in the present work in a slightly modified form.

In this article, Annika Persson presents a survey carried out by the Council of Europe in preparation for the Oslo seminar. The article is based on replies from thirty-six of the forty-eight countries party to the European Cultural Convention, and for each country, replies were solicited from students, representatives of higher education institutions and ministries responsible for higher education.

The survey covered three broad areas of concern:

- formal provision for student representation in higher education governance as reflected in national legislation;
- other provisions for student participation in higher education governance;
- actual practices of student participation.

The survey confirmed that student participation is a feature of higher education governance in Europe, and that the attitude to student

---

[2] For further information on this seminar, see http://siu.no/vev.nsf/o/SIUs+Conferences-BolognaOslo. For further information on the Bologna Process aiming to establish a European Higher Education Area by 2010, see http://www.bologna-bergen2005.no/

participation is positive in all groups surveyed. In fact, most respondents, regardless of the group to which they belonged, felt that student participation should be further increased. The survey did find some divergence in provision between countries and between levels of governance. In the latter sense, student participation is particularly well provided for at faculty and institutional level, somewhat less at department/institute level and even less at national level. In this case, however, the equation may be slightly different, in that the political mandate at national level is more clearly given by the voters to the national assembly and the ministry as a general political mandate, which may or may not include a platform on higher education issues. Even where there is no formal provision for student participation in higher education governance at national level, however, in many countries there seems to be considerable informal consultation between the ministry and the relevant student organisations.

While formal provision for student participation is generally assured, there seems to be a serious problem with actual student commitment to participation. While finding candidates to run for elective office does not seem to be a problem – perhaps with certain exceptions at department/institute level – raising sufficient interest in the student body to actually bring a majority of students to cast a vote in student elections is a different matter altogether. In some cases, voter turnout may even be so low as to raise questions about the actual representativity of student members of the higher education governance bodies.

Therefore, stimulating actual student participation rather than improving formal provision for participation would seem to be the steepest challenge in this area. This may be linked to a lack of information, not so much because the relevant information is unavailable but because it is difficult to get across. The problem of information overflow and of providing targeted information to relevant groups is hardly limited to higher education governance, but it is an important one none the less.

However, the challenge extends well beyond a lack of information to disenchantment with the political process in society at large and a focus on the private rather than the public sphere of life.[3] This places higher education governance in the larger context of society development and the role of the university as a societal actor. This is the topic of Frank Plantan's article, which provides an overview of a pilot project undertaken by the Council of Europe in co-operation with a number of higher education organisations from the United States. This project – called the University as Site of Citizenship – was a contribution by the Higher Education and Research Committee of the Council of Europe to the project on Education for Democratic Citizenship. It ultimately involved thirteen European and fifteen North American higher education institutions, and it took an in-depth look at policies and practice at institutional level. The co-operation with the US higher education community is important because awareness of the civic responsibility of higher education is probably greater in the United States than it is in many

---

[3] On this issue, see also Carl Boggs: *The End of Politics,* New York: The Guilford Press, 2000.

European countries, as is manifested in the Wingspread Declaration and the President's Fourth of July Declaration.[4]

In view of the different focus and methodology of this project and the survey presented in Annika Persson's article, it is interesting to note that where they address the same issues, the outcomes point in the same direction. Thus, Frank Plantan maintains that "[f]ormal and statutory provisions for shared governance, transparency of decision making and protection of faculty and student rights are often at odds with reality and actual practices". He points out that lack of information as well as a sense of disempowerment – the feeling that higher education institutions are run by a small group of people and that even student representatives are out of touch with the majority of students – may in part explain the lack of participation.

However, Plantan also points to a lack of understanding on the part of both faculty and students of the role of the university as an actor in democratic society. Many members of the academic community tend to think of the university in terms that bear an eerie resemblance to the ivory tower. At best, they tend to consider the civic role of higher education as a secondary mission, at worst as an infringement upon or dilution of the university's real mission. This leads to what Frank Plantan terms "fragmentation", where students and staff perceive an insurmountable wall between their role in higher education and their lives as citizens. This is very much at odds with the vision of intellectual commitment as something that transcends disciplinary boundaries and extends to all aspects of life, to which Plantan adds the assertion that "student participation in university governance and in asserting or understanding their rights as students are characterised by a *pervasive passivity* bordering on indifference".

In the fourth article, Sergiu Musteață, Angela Garabagiu and I describe an example of good practice in which students and staff have sought to develop their university as a site of citizenship by elaborating a student charter. It is particularly interesting to note that this example, which originates from the project on Education for Democratic Citizenship, stems from one of the Council of Europe's newer member states, Moldova. A group of students and teachers at the Ion Creangă State Pedagogical University sought to spell out students' rights and obligations in terms of a charter, which is not legally binding, but which should be seen as a code of good practice. While some of the provisions of the charter are best understandable with a knowledge of the specific situation of Moldovan higher education, most of the charter has universal relevance and should be seen as a good example of adapting European standards to a local context.

The charter takes as its point of departure that democratic culture is developed through participation and practice, and that the rights of students go beyond a right to attend lectures. The charter intended to raise students' awareness of their rights and responsibilities and, also, to help them experience democratic participation. Therefore, both the final product – the charter – and the process of its development and approval were important.

---

[4] Further details and links to both declarations will be found in Frank Plantan's article.

Starting with general provisions, such as students' right to the recognition of their personality and the universal principle of non-discrimination, the charter outlines students' rights and obligations in a number of areas, including democratic and political rights, physical protection, cultural and linguistic rights, legal and administrative rights and economic and social rights, as well as their right to fair recognition of qualifications earned abroad. Not least, the student charter underlines that "official sources" have an obligation to provide students with adequate information on the life of the institution. This provision is clearly intended to remedy what has been perceived as a major problem in the Moldovan higher education system. The charter also addresses a number of other issues such as employment and student living conditions. Some of these issues are clearly beyond the legal competence of both student organisations and higher education institutions, but the charter still has great value as a moral statement. In addition, its contents as well as its form make it a very valuable source for those in positions of appropriate authority who might wish to transform the provisions of the charter into binding legal obligations through modifications of the relevant rules and regulations.

The appendix reproduces the full text of the Moldovan Student Charter, translated from the original Romanian. This text has also been published separately, in Romanian, English and French, in a work issued jointly by the Council of Europe (the project on Education for Democratic Citizenship), the Ion Creangă State Pedagogical University and the Student League of this university.[5]

Together, the topics addressed in this book show the diversity as well as the importance of the university as an actor in democratic society, both in its own right and as the Alma Mater of many citizens of Europe over the next generations. This has been one of the key roles of the university since the institution was founded in the Middle Ages but, as society itself, this role has taken a new form over the centuries. As Europe has moved from elite to mass higher education, the civic role of the university is more important than ever. This role must be one of teaching and learning through active participation, and it must avoid the pitfalls of exaggerated political correctness. To be effective, missionaries on behalf of democratic culture, universities must lead by example and by learning rather than by teaching or preaching. Mass higher education faces many of the same problems as modern mass society, the least of which is a loss of interest in the public sphere and a concentration on the private sphere; a lack of faith in the importance of working for the community and not only the private good. This is no small challenge, but it is one to which higher education must rise. Failing to do so could have detrimental consequences for the next generation of Europeans. Hopefully this book will be a contribution, however modest, to developing the university as a site of citizenship.

---

[5] In an edition issued in Chişinău in 2003 (ISBN 9975-927-10-6).

Higher education governance and democratic participation: the university and democratic culture

Sjur Bergan

Background and purpose

As a part of the preparation for its follow-up Bologna seminar on Student Participation in Higher Education Governance (Oslo 12-14 June 2003), the Norwegian Ministry of Education, Research and Church Affairs commissioned a report from the Council of Europe to survey the state of affairs with regard to formal provision for student participation as well as actual practice. This survey was conducted by Annika Persson, mainly during her period as a trainee at the Council's Higher Education and Research Division in autumn 2002, with some support from Per Nyborg as Chair of the Council's Higher Education and Research Committee (CD-ESR) and myself. This survey, which Annika Persson completed after she returned to her permanent position in the Swedish Ministry of Education, is included as a separate article in the present work.

The purpose of the present article is to put the findings of this survey in a broader context and draw on other kinds of experience, in particular a pilot project on the University as Site of Citizenship carried out by the CD-ESR in co-operation with a consortium of US higher education institutions and NGOs in 2000-01.[6]

Higher education and society

Higher education institutions are an important part of, and play an important role in, society. The institutions are societies unto themselves, but they are also part of the larger society. If they remained only societies unto themselves, higher education institutions would be locked up in the proverbial ivory tower and their future would most likely be considerably shorter than their past. On the other hand, higher education institutions, without keeping some distance from society at large, would run a serious risk of losing their capacity to reason in terms of principle, or to take a long-term view somewhat detached from the immediate issues of the day, and to identify sustainable solutions to the most serious and long-term challenges facing our society.

The CD-ESR pilot project on the University as Site of Citizenship identified four sets of issues in which higher education institutions have a role to play,

---

[6] The final report, written by Dr Frank Plantan of the University of Pennsylvania is also include in this volume.

as institution and/or through their individual members, that is, the academic community of scholars and students:

- institutional decision making;
- institutional life in a wider sense, including the study process;
- higher education institutions as multicultural societies;
- higher education institutions in their relationship and interaction with the wider society.

While this seminar focused on higher education governance, I will to some extent also draw on the other dimensions identified by the project on the University as Site of Citizenship where this seems relevant.

Higher education governance

Student participation as defined by the Oslo seminar is an aspect of the broader area of higher education governance, so it may be useful to recall that higher education governance is at the heart of the Bologna Process and will be a key feature of the European Higher Education Area to be set up by 2010. To an extent, this is taken for granted, and many institutional representatives and higher education policy makers refer to academic freedom and institutional autonomy – or sometimes a mixture of the two – as if these were obvious features of higher education in Europe, freedoms earned at the dawn of time and destined to be with us until some distant academic sunset.

Yet reality, as so often, is slightly more complicated, even if there is general agreement on the need for autonomous institutions. However, once we start asking what this actually means, consensus breaks down as the level of precision increases. Autonomy is often referred to as "institutional", sometimes as "university", but the question of whether there are differences between the two or whether we need to develop a more nuanced view is rarely asked. Similarly, autonomy is often thought of in legal terms, but even where autonomy from ministries is guaranteed by law and honoured in practice, no institution can be an island unto itself. Institutions are influenced by the expectations and financial contributions of other actors, whether these be ministries and other public authorities, private companies or the somewhat imprecise animal normally referred to as public opinion. Institutions not only *are* influenced by their surroundings, but they *should be*, at least to an extent. The problem, then, is not one of principle, but of finding the right balance.

Similarly, we tend to take it for granted that universities or higher education institutions – again, there tends to be lack of precision – are headed by an elected official who goes by many different names according to the context but who internationally tends to be referred to as the rector, and governed by a representative body elected by the academic community, typically by various combinations of the words university, academic, senate and council.

Recently, however, a good number of universities have welcomed representatives who are not members of the academic community on their governing bodies – or they have been forced to accept such representatives, as the case may be. These representatives underline the fact that universities are a part of the larger society, that they have a duty to this society and that they both contribute to and are influenced by it. Nor is this really a new development. It is not the phenomenon of interdependence between higher education and society at large that is new, but rather the form this interdependence may take.[7] Some higher education institutions now even have institutional leaders hired on fixed-term contracts and often recruited from the outside rather than rectors elected by the academic community. So far, there has been little debate on the implications of these developments on our concept of higher education governance. The same, albeit to a slightly lesser extent, holds true for the relationship between the higher education institution and its faculties, which is a particularly pertinent issue in several countries emanating from former Yugoslavia.

Student participation: banging on open doors?

The topic for the Oslo seminar was the specific part of higher education governance that has to do with the participation and contribution of students. This, also, we perhaps tend to take for granted, so it may be useful to remember that times have indeed been changing. This is true for the Bologna Process as well as for higher education governance proper.

Students, represented by ESIB,[8] are now observers on the follow-up and preparatory groups and active contributors to the Bologna Process, so it is easy to forget that student representation was neither foreseen nor much talked about at the original 1999 Bologna Conference. Students, in fact, did not move to centre stage until the Prague Conference in 2001, when the President of ESIB spoke to the ministers and the latter stated that "the involvement of universities and other higher education institutions and of students as competent, active and constructive partners in the establishment and shaping of a European Higher Education Area is needed and welcomed". In the Prague Communiqué, ministers also "affirmed that students should participate in and influence the organisation and content of education at universities and other higher education institutions" and that "students are full members of the higher education community". In moving from observers to key actors in the Bologna Process in two years, the students did of course have the support of many ministers of education, some of whom actively pushed for a stronger student participation in the Bologna Process. In this way, the process would be in better conformity with the situation in most of its constituent parties. Nevertheless, it may be worth

---

[7] For an early example, see J. K. Hyde: "Universities and cities in medieval Italy" in Thomas Bender (ed.): *The University and the City. From Medieval Origins to the Present,* New York, Oxford University Press, 1988. For a broad view of the university heritage, see Nuria Sanz and Sjur Bergan (eds): *The Heritage of European Universities*, Strasbourg: Council of Europe Publishing, 2002.
[8] National Unions of Students in Europe (http://www.esib.org)

noting that at least one respondent to the survey carried out by the Council of Europe for the Oslo seminar underlined the need for stronger student participation in the follow-up structures of the Bologna Process.

Also in the governance of higher education institutions, we are used to taking student representation and student participation so much for granted that it is easy to forget that in most European countries, this representation in its current form is little more than a generation old. If the Bologna Process is the most important reform of higher education in Europe since the immediate aftermath of 1968, we should keep in mind that this previous wave of reform was very different. Both reform movements are about adapting higher education to a changing society, but whereas the Bologna Process was started at the initiative of ministers, 1968 was started by students in the street, and one of their main demands was the need for a stronger student influence not just on higher education governance, but on university life in general, with issues ranging from student representation on university senates and improved access for disadvantaged groups to less restrictive rules on gender relations in university dorms.[9]

Today, there is a feeling that the formal aspect of student representation has largely been settled, but I am not aware of any previous large-scale survey of the facts. Second, there is also a feeling that even if the formal right to representation has been secured, students' actual use of that right is far from satisfactory. To put it crudely, while previous generations of students fought for representation, there is an impression that the current student generation does not make much use of the rights gained. However, it would be helpful to know whether this impression is in fact substantiated by facts and, if so, why present-day students are to a large extent disconnected at least from institutional governance and perhaps even from institutional life. Third, it would be useful to know something about student perceptions of their influence on higher education governance, and this might even offer a clue as to why actual participation is as it is. These, then, are the three topics addressed by the survey.

Formal student representation in higher education governance

What is normally thought of as student participation in higher education governance, namely formal provision for student representation on the governing bodies of higher education institutions, seems to be a general feature of higher education in Europe. Representatives of only two countries indicate that there is no legal provision for student representation on the governing bodies of the institutions. However, legal regulation of such representation at faculty and, even more so, at department level is less common, and at national level provision for student representation is found only in a narrow majority of cases. On closer reflection, however, this may

---

[9] Didier Fischer: *L'histoire des étudiants en France de 1945 à nos jours*, Paris: Flammarion, 2000, pp. 288-290. This book provides an interesting and readable overview of the development of the student movement in France since 1945.

not be surprising. At institutional, faculty and department level, higher education governance takes place within a clearly defined framework of institutional self-governance with clearly defined partners.[10] At national level, the framework is less clear, as both ministries and national assemblies have a general political mandate. It would be interesting to see whether a consultative framework has been developed, to what extent this is formalised and to what extent students have a voice in bodies such as national rectors' conferences.

If we start scratching below the surface to find out what student representation means in somewhat greater detail, we see that in the great majority of cases, regulations stipulate that between one in ten and one in five of all members of higher education governing bodies be students. In no case do students elect a majority of the representatives on the governing body, and in a number of cases student representation seems to be below 10%.

However, it is not enough to be present, it is also of interest to know what competence – in this case in the legal sense of the term – student representatives actually have. In the vast majority of cases, student representatives are full members of the governing body in the sense that they have the right to speak and vote on all issues that come before the board. However, in eight countries whose representatives replied to the survey, student voting rights were limited to issues that seem to be considered of most immediate concern to the students, while they are not allowed to vote on issues that concern staff appointments, administrative and finance issues, curricula or issues relating to the granting of doctoral degrees. While this relates to only eight countries covered by the survey, it seems worthwhile to dwell on the issue as it raises an important question of principle.

There are two ways of interpreting such differentiated voting rights: they are either differentiated according to the stake students are perceived to have in the issues, or the differentiation is made according to competence – here in the sense of knowledge of the issues. In both cases, it is difficult to see why students should not vote on financial issues. If real competence is the line of argument, the formal argument for limiting voting rights on the granting of doctoral degrees to staff members who have earned this qualification themselves may seem evident, but it overlooks two factors: first, that the governing bodies would tend to act on, and in the great majority of cases follow the advice of, a committee of experts appointed for the occasion, and second, that holding a doctoral qualification in one academic area does not necessarily mean that one is similarly qualified in other areas. A professor of business administration does not necessarily have a comparative advantage in assessing a doctoral thesis in astrophysics.[11]

---

[10] Although the newer development with increased external representation has been referred to above.

[11] I actually defended this point of view as a student representative on the academic senate of the University of Oslo in 1981-82, in a newspaper debate with a former rector of the Veterinary College.

It therefore seems safe to say that, with the exception of voting rights on some issues that come before the governing bodies, student representation is assured from a formal point of view. This is particularly true at institutional level, but it also largely holds true at faculty and, to a somewhat lesser extent, at department level. At the national level, however, the representation is less well-established in formal terms. These findings coincide with the findings of the pilot project on the University as Site of Citizenship.[12]

Student politics?

One issue at the crossroads of formal provision and actual practice concerns how student representatives are identified and elected. In fact, elections are almost universal: the survey revealed five countries in which student representatives are appointed rather than elected, and in all but one of these the appointment is made by the student union. In the one case where the university or faculty appoints student representatives, a legal change seems to be on its way. One can of course ask to what extent the student unions making the appointments are representative of the student body at large, but that is a question of practice rather than formal provision.

The most serious question arising in this area is what kind of student organisations are allowed, and in particular whether these may be linked to political parties. These are generally referred to as "political" student organisations, but it may be worth underlining that politics is about organising and governing societies, and that no society can do without politics or a measure of political actors and organisations, even if these are not political parties in the conventional sense of the term. No society can be governed "apolitically", notwithstanding the claims of certain dictators to this effect.

Representatives from fifteen of the countries that replied to the questionnaire state that "political student organisations" are illegal in higher education institutions. While the term "political" was not defined in the questionnaire, it was intended to mean "affiliated with a political party", and this is also how the question was understood by the respondents. Of the fifteen countries that reported prohibitions of student organisations affiliated with political parties, all but two are to be found in central and eastern Europe. This is consistent with the findings of the pilot project on the University as Site of Citizenship, which states:

> "Another structural characteristic of universities is the legal and administrative prescriptions regarding organised political activity within the university. Many institutions in this study, particularly those in transitional societies or who have recently experienced violent conflict are attempting to respond to new statutory and constitutional

---

[12] Except that, since this project focused on institutional practice, representation at national level was not addressed by the project.

arrangements. They are struggling with redefining roles and responsibilities while simultaneously dealing with basic issues of meeting their educational mission within tight fiscal and budgetary constraints."[13]

This prohibition may perhaps be understandable in the light of the recent past of most of the countries where the ban is enforced, where political organisations served the needs of the regime, both in controlling academic activity and in recruiting "reliable" future party workers. From a thoroughly "politicised" but tightly controlled system, the temptation to turn to one without both politics and control is great, but the question is still whether this is feasible and desirable.

An additional reason for such a ban is the view that students should "concentrate on their education". This view was expressed to researchers in the pilot project, where:

"[m]ost sites reported that university administrators and many faculty considered many aspects of citizenship and democracy to be entirely a *personal matter* such as decisions to vote, to volunteer in the community, to participate in campus organisations, or to engage in political debate and, therefore, not within their ken nor responsibilities as teachers and scholars."[14]

This represents a narrow view of the purpose of higher education that is limited to the role of academic disciplines and that leaves little room for the social function of education, such as developing the ability to live as active citizens in a democratic society.

In a somewhat narrower sense, there is also a desire to keep contentious issues off campus, so as not to make higher education institutions battlefields for groups with sharply divergent views on issues often linked to conflicts that divide the societies concerned, such as ethnic or religious conflicts. In a different context, this view was expressed by the principal of a school in Strasbourg with a high number of foreign students, who publicly made it clear that she would never tolerate students bringing any conflict between their home countries into the school yard or classroom. An example in the opposite sense is, however, provided by Queen's University, Belfast, which has for a long time made consistent efforts to accommodate members of both major religious communities in Northern Ireland and which has pioneered many of the measures that made the current Peace Process possible.

While a limitation of the activities of political parties, or organisations linked to these, in higher education institutions may be understandable on the basis of past experience, the limitation may nevertheless be questioned on grounds of principle as well as of efficiency.

---

[13] The final report by Dr Frank Plantan, CD-ESR (2002) 2, p. 19.
[14] Ibid., p. 13.

The actual practice of student participation

If the survey as well as the pilot project confirm that formal rights to student participation are now almost universal, what use do students make of these rights? Do the formalities work as intended? These questions can be asked from at least two angles: first, is the general student body sufficiently active and interested to give its representatives legitimacy and, second, are student representatives effective once elected, or are they rather helping institutions fulfil the formal requirements of representation without having any real influence on institutional policies? The latter question also concerns how students perceive their influence, to which we will return shortly.

The survey carried out for the Oslo seminar shows that in general it is possible to find motivated candidates to run for office, even if this seems more difficult at department level than at higher levels. It also shows that candidates run either as individuals or on tickets not affiliated with political parties and that the degree of organised politicking increases with the level of representation. In other words, candidates are more likely to run as individuals at department level than at faculty level, and so on. The replies indicate that a plurality of candidates run as individuals at department level, whereas at faculty level a plurality of, and at an institutional level a majority of, candidates run as a representive of an organisation.

This far, the results look good, but this changes when we examine voter turnout in student elections. Although turnout varies considerably, it tends to be low. The overwhelming majority of respondents indicate that voter turnout is in one of the three lowest percentage ranges indicated (0-15%, 16-30% or 31-45%). Therefore, most of the time, less than half the student population elects those representing the whole student body, and in most cases voter turnout is actually one in three or less.

These figures indicate that something is wrong, and they are borne out by the pilot project on the University as Site of Citizenship. This project not only confirms the low voter turnout, indicated as 8-10% at two of the institutions participating in that study, but also indicates some interesting elements of explanation. It is hardly surprising that one important part of the explanation is that students feel under pressure to complete their studies as soon as possible and with as good results as possible, and that they therefore find little time for institutional life. In fact, not finding the time to do something normally indicates giving it a low priority, so participating in and contributing to institutional life in general and institutional governance in particular does not seem to be a priority for many, perhaps most, students.

An interesting observation concerns institutions in countries in which a period of great political conflict and tension has been followed by a period of normalisation. In these cases – exemplified by institutions in Albania and Lithuania where the most intense period was in the early 1990s and in Greece where it occured around 1974 – student mobilisation was strong in the period of crisis and the immediate aftermath, both in general terms and relating to involvement with institutional governance. However, once the crisis blew over and democratic governance was established, student interest declined considerably. This "democratic fatigue" corresponds to the experience of many institutions in western Europe, where student interest declined once student representation had been secured in the aftermath of 1968. Thus, while it seems possible to mobilise students for a "great cause", it seems much more difficult to maintain a sustained interest in and commitment to institutional life and governance.

A second major point that arises from the survey is that even where formal provision is absent, there may be informal consultations at national level, where in many cases there is no formalised representation. In most countries there seems to be regular contact between the ministry responsible for higher education and student representatives, typically the national student union. This may be unsatisfactory from a formal point of view, but such contacts can nevertheless help students wield considerable influence.

Perceptions of influence

If the formal representation of students in higher education governance is generally provided for but student interest in electing representatives is low, is there a connection with students' perceptions of their influence on university life in general and higher education governance in particular?

The survey did in fact not ask directly whether students feel they can influence university governance, and the selection of respondents was not such that this question would have made much sense. Since the respondents were mostly engaged in university governance, directly or indirectly, as members of student unions, academics or ministry officials, the answers would presumably have been skewed. The survey did, however, ask more nuanced questions about perceived influence, in that it asked respondents to identify the areas and levels where they feel that student influence was the strongest and weakest.

All groups of respondents feel that students have the most influence on what may be seen as "immediate issues", such as social issues, the learning environment and educational content, in addition to the somewhat less decipherable category "institutional level generally". At the other end of the scale we find "hard" issues such as budget issues and criteria for recruiting teaching staff as well as on student admission. Budget policies are clearly a key instrument for implementing institutional policy, and as such they are also of immediate concern to students. In terms of level, most respondents feel that the student voice is more easily heard at institutional and faculty level than at the levels immediately above or below, that is, national and department level.

Another indirect indication of student influence is that a large majority of respondents in all categories feel that student influence should be increased. That 90% of student respondents think so is perhaps no great surprise, but it is interesting to note that 72% of academic and 70% of ministry respondents share this view.

Again, the findings of the survey are borne out by those of the pilot project on the University as Site of Citizenship, where researchers asked more direct questions about whether or not students felt they had influence on institutional life. The answers are, in fact, not very encouraging, even at institutions that in their own view make substantial efforts at consulting with and involving their students. The summary of the study states this very directly: "Formal and statutory provisions for shared governance, transparency of decision making and protection of faculty and student rights are often at odds with reality and actual practices".[15]

In the body of the study, this is made more explicit. At one university, respondents felt that a few individuals continue to dominate the decision-making process, while at several universities from different parts of Europe the feeling was that students are rarely if ever consulted and that there are no public hearings on university decisions.

These views are clearly linked to the issue of information given to students, which is felt to be insufficient, something that is reflected in the study carried out by Annika Persson for the Oslo seminar as well as in the project on the University as Site of Citizenship. A dictum has it that "information is power", and information is an important condition for participation as active citizens in a democratic society. At the same time, we know that information is a difficult issue in many areas of modern society. In many contexts, the problem is not lack of information per se, but lack of reliable and targeted information.[16]

In several countries, there is still a strong tradition that senior faculty "decides everything". Where there is student involvement, there is at the same time a feeling that this does not lead to many concrete results, and that student representatives, while a part of the process, have little influence on it. There is also a perception that student politics is run by a small elite without much contact with "normal" students. This, perhaps, echoes a frequent complaint about politics in general, but it is a serious challenge to student representatives, politicians in society at large and indeed to all members of society. While it is certainly not difficult to find examples of politicians who deserve our scorn, society at whatever level is in serious trouble if it becomes fashionable to despise politics, because it would then be fashionable not to care about how our own societies are run. History has too many examples of what such attitudes of complacence can lead to, from all sides of the political spectrum.[17]

---

[15] Ibid., p. 12.

[16] The lack of clear and targeted information was one of the main issues raised at the follow-up Bologna seminar on Recognition Issues in the Bologna Process, organised by the Council of Europe and the Portuguese authorities in Lisbon on 11-12 April 2002. See in particular the articles by Stephen Adam and Chantal Kaufmann in Sjur Bergan (ed.) *Recognition Issues in the Bologna Process,* Strasbourg: Council of Europe Publishing, 2003.

[17] For an interesting, if depressing, example of the political thought of a right wing military regime, see Augusto Pinochet Ugarte: *Política, politiquería, demagogia,* Santiago de Chile: Editorial Renacimiento,1983.

In this project, there even seems to be a consistent difference in the way respondents addressed the issue of perceptions of influence: student respondents tended to emphasise what they perceived as real influence – or lack of it – whereas administrators tended to focus on formal student participation. Therefore, it is possible that the different groups did in fact not answer the same question, even if the same questions were asked of all. It is also interesting to note that students at three universities tended to have a more positive view of their influence. The foremost of these was Queen's University, Belfast, which has not only played a significant role in the Northern Ireland Peace Process – something that could hardly be done without consultation – but where the university leadership at the time the study was carried out was particularly known for collegiate leadership. As the study puts it, "[t]his not only sets a 'tone' for proper democratic demand and problem solving, such leadership typically directs the university mission towards meeting the objectives of civic education and democracy in its education programmes".

Why should students influence institutional governance?

One may perhaps have expected this question to be asked at the outset of this article, but I have preferred to survey facts and perceptions before entering into normative arguments. The survey does, incidentally, provide guidance also on this point, as respondents were asked why they felt – as the majority of them did – that student influence should be strengthened. The replies focused on the role of students as stakeholders in higher education; from many respondents' points of view they are even the main stakeholders.

I will take these arguments one step further and consider the role of students in somewhat more detail. My point of departure is that there is an increasing tendency to think of students as clients. This paradigm does, however, have profound implications for the relationship between students and the institutions at which they study. Clients essentially expect a number of defined services from a provider, and they would normally take little interest in the provider as long as these services are delivered as expected at an affordable price and acceptable quality, according to the contract, in commercial terms. There may be some exceptions, such as boycotts of companies refusing to hire ethnic or religious minorities, but these remain exceptions. If client expectations are not met, most clients respond by looking for the desired services elsewhere rather than by attempting to take control of the provider to make it deliver the services as stipulated or desired.

Taken to the extreme, the idea of students as clients contradicts the more traditional idea of students as members of the academic community.[18] The idea of community does not exclude the possibility of there being conflicting opinions about the purpose and standard of education, but it sees the

---

[18] This notion was underlined by the Bologna ministers in their Prague Communiqué.

students as participants rather than as receivers or buyers of a final product. As members of the academic community, students share a responsibility for their education and for the institution that provides the framework for this education. If the education is unsatisfactory, the response would be to try to improve the institution and the education it provides rather than to go elsewhere.

In real life, none of these extremes will be readily found. Students do legitimately have specific expectations for their education (in terms of quality, profile, price, conditions of study, etc.) and few students can afford to spend years of their life trying to improve an institution if what it gives them does not come reasonably close to their expectations, especially if other institutions – or alternative experiences outside higher education – can better meet their expectations and needs. Most students embark on higher education because the qualifications they earn will help them reach their goals later in life. Academic mobility, that is, getting students to move between higher education institutions, is of course also an important policy goal for higher education institutions as well as governments and international organisations.

However, students also see themselves as members of a community, as participants. While most students have utilitarian reasons for taking higher education, few would think that higher education does not also have an intrinsic value. I think it is worth emphasising that while much of the current discussion on higher education, inside as well as outside the Bologna Process, focuses on its role in relation to the labour market, we should take into account the full range of purposes of higher education. In my view, these are at least four:

- preparation for the labour market;
- preparation for life as active citizens in a democratic society;
- personal development;
- development and maintenance of an advanced knowledge base.

Students should have clear expectations of higher education institutions – expectations that are not always met – but they should also see themselves as a part of the institution. That may not always mean they identify very strongly with the institution as such[19] but they do at least identify with groups within the institution, such as the student body as a whole, a specific department, students in a specific department, etc. This identification is not and should not be uncritical, and students should make demands on their institutions and teachers, but if they no longer consider themselves as a part of the institution and the academic community, I believe higher education in Europe will have a very serious problem. In a sense, students must be

---

[19] It may even be that some models of higher education tend to encourage a stronger institutional identification than others. It is at least a superficial impression that US students identify more closely with their institutions than many continental European students do.

24

members of an "imagined community" [20] that crosses national and institutional borders.

If we believe that higher education has a role in developing the democratic culture without which democratic institutions cannot function and democratic societies cannot exist, it is, as the pilot project on the University as Site of Citizenship points out, important to realise that these attitudes cannot be developed simply by seeing and learning. Doing is of the essence. Therefore, students must be encouraged to participate, and they must feel that their participation has an impact.

At least two caveats may be in order, and they both have to do with the democratic character of higher education institutions. The first is whether higher education institutions and their staff and students are necessarily democratic, and it is, unfortunately, not difficult for any of us to think of examples to the contrary. Here, I will therefore only point to a few selective examples. Many of the Council of Europe's member states – and current or future participants in the Bologna Process – in their recent higher education history have no shortage of examples of how communist regimes used higher education institutions for their own purposes and how many staff members and students played along. The judges at show trials [21] were graduates of law faculties, and party membership was no disadvantage in securing staff appointments or places of study, provided the membership was in the "right" party. In the Germany of the 1920s and 1930s, most university teachers were nostalgic for pre-First World War elitist society and lukewarm to the Weimar Republic and even if the majority of them were not Nazi supporters, it was only a minority that fought actively against the Nazi regime. [22] Even as anti-intellectual a movement as the Nazi party had its student organisations and student supporters. In Portugal, the main leaders of the Salazar regime had their roots at the University of Coimbra. [23] In Chile, the Pinochet regime received strong support from a group of economists at the Universidad Católica who had some of their formative experience at the University of Chicago and who were therefore known as the Chicago boys. They were the moving force behind the economic liberalism of the Pinochet regime and they were largely unconcerned by its human rights abuses. [24] Nor is this a preogative of the undemocratic right. On the undemocratic left, we find students and staff in Maoist movements in Europe, and a little further afield, the leader and ideologue of the Peruvian terrorist movement *Sendero*

---

[20] The term "imagined community" is normally used in discussions of nationalism and was coined by the political scientist Benedict Anderson in his *Imagined Communities: Reflections on the Origin and Spread of Nationalism*, London: Verso, 1983, but, if used with care, the term may be fitting also for other kinds of communities.

[21] See for example Ulrich Mählert: *Kleine Geschichte der DDR*, Munich: Verlag C. H. Beck, 1999, esp. pp. 62-65.

[22] See Notker Hammerstein : "Universities and democratisation: an historical perspective. The case of Germany" (Paper written for a Council of Europe conference on Universities and Democratisation, Warsaw, 29-31 January 1992, reference DECS-HE 91/97).

[23] Cf. Luis Reis Torgal: *A Universidade e o Estado Novo*, Coimbra: Livreria Minerva Editora, 1999.

[24] For an excellent analysis, see Carlos Huneus: *El régimen de Pinochet*, Santiago de Chile: Editorial Sudamericana, 2001.

luminoso, Abimael Guzmán, was a philosophy lecturer at the University of Ayacucho.[25]

The point is of course not that universities, scholars or students are inherently undemocratic. For each of the examples mentioned, counter examples can be found. In central and eastern Europe, the movements that ultimately brought down the communist regimes were also often led by academics, and immediately after the political changes in the early 1990s, some university departments were decimated because many of their members had been democratically elected to parliament. Germany not only had Nazi students, but also student and staff resistants who paid with their lives, such as the Scholl siblings and other members of the Weisse Rose. Academics played an important role in the opposition to the Salazar regime, especially from the 1960s onwards; voices such as José Afonso gave artistic expression to this through the *fado de Coimbra*.[26] Chilean academics played an important part in the opposition to the Pinochet regime and Maoist student movements were not unopposed even in the immediate aftermath of 1968. Under the Milošević regime, which in 1998 passed a particularly repressive higher education law that was implemented by government-appointed rectors and deans, academic and democratic values were upheld by members of the academic community who often lost their jobs and who were in many cases members of the Alternative Academic Education Network.

The point is, rather, that politically, higher education institutions and their members are not much better or worse than society at large, and while they may tend to phrase their arguments in more theoretical terms, democracy must be maintained through both reflection and practice, on campus as elsewhere in society.

The second caveat is whether universities should be democratic and, if they should, in what way.

University governance – how democratic is it?

A universal feature of the legal regulations is that students hold a substantial yet minority number of seats on the governing bodies. In other words, seats on the governing bodies are not distributed according to numerical strength. The democratic principle of one person, one vote is, then, not the norm in higher education institutions, where the votes (or number of representatives) of three groups are weighted according to their perceived roles in institutional life. Academic staff, perceived as having the main responsibility for the key missions of the university – teaching and research – in general elect a majority of the members of the decision-making bodies, whereas

---

[25] An enjoyable fictional account probably modelled on the *Sendero luminoso* is Mario Vargas Llosa: *Historia de Mayta*.
[26] See Maria da Fátima Silva: "The University of Coimbra and its traditions at the beginning of a new millennium" in Nuria Sanz and Sjur Bergan (eds): *The Heritage of European Universities*, Strasbourg: Council of Europe Publishing, 2002.

students often elect a larger number of representatives than the administrative and technical staff (although students are not better represented if, rather than the total number of representatives, one measures the number of voters per representative).

Votes, then, are weighted according to competence or function in relation to the missions of the university. Is this in contradiction to democratic principles, or is it simply that it is possible to define competence or function in the context of the university but not in that of civil society, in which all members have an equal stake? It may be noted that such weighting of votes is not unique to universities. It is found in a variety of contexts ranging from commercial companies (voting in relation to the number of shares owned) to diocesan councils (with separate representation of clergy and laity) [27] and international organisations. [28] It may also be noted that attempts at introducing competence tests, such as literacy tests, into general elections are generally seen as undemocratic and even as attempts to keep less favoured groups from voting.[29] Weighted representation of specific groups is generally regarded as undemocratic but is none the less seen as acceptable in certain circumstances, generally in terms of geography[30] or to increase the representation of an under-represented group (such as specific quotas for women), to ensure representation of a group whose voice may otherwise not be heard[31] or to ensure a modus vivendi in a highly conflictual society.[32]

It should also be noted that academic staff, students and administrative and technical staff are not necessarily homogenous groups given to bloc voting. Members of each of these groups may influence members of other groups by their arguments, and a majority may consist of some academic staff, students and administrative and technical staff. It is even conceivable that a majority of academic staff may be voted down by a coalition of students and administrative and technical staff with a minority of academic staff representatives. Incidentally, the survey indirectly underlined this point in that respondents from the same country did not always agree on their interpretation of the facts, or even on what the facts are.

---

[27] It should be noted that neither commercial companies nor diocesan councils, while concerned with a measure of representativity, necessarily aim to be democratic.

[28] In the United Nations, five countries are permanent members of the Security Council and may veto decisions of this body. In most other contexts, including the General Assembly of the United Nations, international organisations are generally run on the principle that each country has one vote, regardless of the size of its population, so that the basic unit of representation is the country or government rather than the individual.

[29] One example among many is the literacy tests used in the US Deep South in parts of the twentieth century.

[30] In many countries, there are fewer votes behind each representative elected from rural than from urban districts. In Switzerland, the provision that a proposal put to a national referendum must win a majority not only in the referendum at large, but also in a specified number of cantons, tends to weight voting in favour of the less populous cantons.

[31] The institutionalised representation of the Maori population in the New Zealand Parliament, the quota of representatives of the Serb population and other minorities in the Kosovo legislative assembly or the existence of the Sámi parliament, an advisory body, in Norway are three examples.

[32] Examples include the presidency of Bosnia and Herzegovina, with one representative of each major ethnic community, and the increasingly contested provisions made in the Lebanese constitution, with a Maronite President, a Sunni Prime Minister and a Shiite Speaker of Parliament.

The way ahead

At least as a preliminary conclusion to our consideration of the formal provision for student representation, it seems reasonable to say that the issue is largely settled, perhaps with the exception of representation at national level in a good number of countries and in more limited cases of the right of student representatives to vote on all issues that come before the governing body. While students have fewer representatives than academic staff, this is justifiable on theoretical grounds, and from a practical point of view, a student representation of 10-30% does not seem to be widely contested.

It is also comforting to see that those who provided input to the Council of Europe study seem to agree on a wide range of issues, including the need for improved information and the desirability of improving student representation in higher education governance. The starting point for our discussion of further action – or for the road map for our way ahead, to use the most recent policy-speak – is therefore a reasonably high level of consensus, at least on the main principles.

If the formalities are settled, what are the issues on which the Bologna Process should focus if student representation is still to be on its agenda?

First, there seems to be an issue concerning the level of representation, which particularly concerns student participation at national level and seems to be an issue of both formal provisions and practice. How can the further development of national higher education systems – and the Bologna Process itself – best benefit from the contribution of students, and how can these important stakeholders gain the same influence they now have at institutional level?

Second, even if student representation is almost universal, we have seen that, in some countries, student representatives cannot vote on all issues. Is this really reasonable? Even if we accept that academic staff may have a stronger representation than students for reasons of competence in the core areas of higher education (teaching, learning and research), is it reasonable that, once the student representation on governing bodies has been determined, students should not speak or vote on all issues brought before these bodies?

A greater challenge is linked to real influence rather than formal representation. These issues may be linked in a vicious circle: if students believe they have little or no interest, why should they participate in governance or even vote? However, if students do not vote, why should they have a greater influence? Here we touch on institutional culture, on the way in which institutions are governed and decisions made, and this is an issue that goes beyond student representation. To what extent should decisions be consensual, and to what extent do institutions need strong leadership?

The answer to this question is not as straightforward as it would seem, and I believe the issue should be considered within the Bologna Process. On the one hand, institutions where staff and students are committed to common goals and common reforms have a considerable advantage over those where no such consensus emerges, and institutional leadership should not be too aloof from the average staff member. The same could of course be said of the relationship between student representatives and the average student. In the project on the University as Site of Citizenship, Queen's University, Belfast, was identified as an institution with an inspirational leadership that achieved considerable results through persuasion. On the other hand, a consensus-oriented governance model can also be a recipe for stalemate under which small groups or certain parts of the university can block any attempt at reform. The situation in many countries of former Yugoslavia, where faculties have an independent legal personality and a correspondingly weak institutional leadership (rectorate), is perhaps an extreme example, but the dilemma is real at many institutions in all parts of Europe.

The question of the relative weight of institutional self-governance and external influence is linked to this. It indirectly concerns student participation but is really an essential aspect of overall institutional governance. The issue is that of defining the stakeholders in higher education and their relative role as well as the relationship between stakeholder interest and their actual higher education competence. To what extent should society at large, which contributes substantially to financing higher education, have a direct say in institutional governance, and who should represent this society at large which strongly resembles the proverbial duck: we recognise it when we see it but it is difficult to define and, I would add, to operationalise. The social partners (employers and trade unions) are important partners also for higher education institutions, but can they alone represent society at large? In most democracies, society is represented by politicians, but is the participation of political parties in higher education governance the right way to go? The material presented here at the very least indicates that views on the role – if any – of party politics at higher education institutions are highly diverse.

This leads me to what is perhaps the greatest challenge of all, namely the low interest that students show in the governance of their higher education institutions and systems. Again, as important as this is for the issue of student representation, I would tend to see this in the context of disenchantment with the political process in society at large as well as the problem of providing clear and targeted information in a society where most people receive far more information than they can possibly absorb, and I have already underlined the seriousness of the issue. Therefore, an important part of the discussion should focus on how we can stimulate students as well as staff to take an active interest not only in their own teaching, learning and research but in the life and governance of their institution and the society of which it is a part. In the classical French tragedies, the ideal was to be loved, but it was better to be hated than to be ignored, and I sometimes wonder if this is not true for higher education governance as well.

I would therefore point to two overall conclusions that, in addition to the questions just raised, should guide the further work within the Bologna Process. First, we need to stimulate interest in and commitment to higher education among those most directly involved: students and staff. Second, however important student participation, it is a part of the overall issue of higher education governance and should, in my view, be considered within this framework.

Last, but not least: governance issues are not a luxury or a concern of the few while the majority of staff and students get on with their work. Rather, they are part and parcel of the contribution of higher education to developing and maintaining the democratic culture without which democratic institutions cannot function, and they are crucial to ensuring that the academic community of scholars and students be not only an imagined community but also a real and healthy one.

Student participation in the governance of higher education in Europe: results of a survey

Annika Persson

Introduction

The Bologna Declaration was signed in 1999 by the ministers responsible for higher education of twenty-nine countries and has the creation of a European Higher Education Area by 2010 as its ultimate objective. The declaration aims at more transparent and mutually recognised systems of higher education in order to increase the mobility and employability of students and staff, as well as promoting the attractiveness of European higher education.

Student participation in the governance of higher education is an important part of the Bologna Process. The Bologna Declaration underlines the importance of educational co-operation across boundaries and across organisations, aiming at developing and strengthening democratic societies.

At the ministerial meeting in Prague in May 2001 the ministers put a stronger emphasis on certain topics within the Bologna Process through the Prague Communiqué, one of these being student participation. Important steps forward were the statement that "students are full members of the higher education community" and the recognition of students as "competent, active and constructive partners" in the establishment and shaping of a European Higher Education Area. Ministers affirmed that students should participate in and influence the organisation and content of education at universities and other higher education institutions. Further student involvement was explicitly mentioned in the Prague Communiqué as one of the themes for the seminars the ministers encouraged the Bologna Follow-Up Group to arrange. The ministers also appreciated the active involvement of the National Unions of Students in Europe (ESIB) in the Bologna Process.

From 12 to 14 June 2003 the Norwegian Ministry of Education and Research held a seminar on the issue of student participation in the governance of higher education. The seminar was held within the framework of the Bologna Process and the topic of student involvement was, as stated above, explicitly mentioned in the Prague Communiqué.

To prepare the seminar, and to try to acquire a better knowledge of the situation in different countries, the Norwegian ministry commissioned the Council of Europe to carry out a survey on student participation in the governance of higher education.

Method and recipients

The survey was carried out through a questionnaire to the three main groups concerned:

- students;
- representatives of higher education institutions (academics);
- ministries responsible for higher education.

The questionnaire was sent to the member organisations of ESIB (the National Unions of Students in Europe). ESIB consists of forty-one full members, four candidates and two consultative members from thirty-five countries.[33] Accordingly, some countries are represented by more than one organisation. The questionnaire was also sent to the national delegations to the Council of Europe's Steering Committee for Higher Education and Research (CD-ESR). The CD-ESR is composed of both government and academic representatives from each of the signatory states to the European Cultural Convention (representing forty-eight countries).[34]

The questionnaire was sent out in mid-October 2002, in English and French, and answers were requested by mid-November. Three reminders were sent out during November.

Student replies were received from twenty-eight countries, which is a large majority of the thirty-five countries in which ESIB had members at the time of the survey. Academic replies were received from twenty-four countries, representing half the number of the countries that received the questionnaire. Ministry replies were received from twenty-one countries (44% of the countries receiving the questionnaire). It should be noted that the respondents sometimes represent only a part of the higher education sector in the country in question and that sometimes they have answered as individuals.

Replies from one or more group representatives were received from a total of thirty-six countries. No answers from any of the three groups represented were received from Albania, Azerbaijan, Bosnia and Herzegovina, France, Ireland, Luxembourg, Poland, the Russian Federation, the Slovak Republic, Ukraine or the United Kingdom.

From twenty-five countries, two or three group representatives answered. In three countries, because of the structure of student organisations at the national level, two student organisations in each country answered. When the number of replies is counted, all of these student answers are included.

The number of answers and therefore countries and groups represented may be limited in some of the questions or alternative answers, especially in questions with many possible alternative responses. Because of this, results

---

[33] See list of members at http://www.esib.org.
[34] See list of signatories at http://www.coe.int.

presented as percentages have been used in the report only where the numbers have been considered large enough not to be misleading when converted into percentages.

It has not been considered methodologically feasible to systematically indicate the number of countries that gave a certain answer, since respondents representing the same country have often provided diverging answers.

Definitions

The survey focuses on the issue of student participation in the *governance* of higher education. Student influence on social issues, housing, etc., are equally important questions, but they are not the main focus of this survey. The issue of governance has been divided into three parts:

- formal provision for student participation in higher education governance based on national legislation;
- other provision for student participation;
- the actual practice of student participation.

The definition of "higher education institution" or "institution" used in the survey covers both universities and other higher education institutions, such as *Fachhochschulen*. They also cover both public and private institutions under national law, even if these institutions may differ in governance regulations.

The term "country" in the report also covers parts of countries or communities where responsibility for higher education is at this level, such as the Flemish and French-speaking communities of Belgium.

When the term "respondents" is referred to, all replies are counted, including the double answers from student organisations in three countries. A "country representative" can be a member of any of the three groups. A "group" refers to one of the three groups receiving the questionnaire: students, academics, ministries.

Main findings

Overall trends

Before entering into the details of the survey, it may be useful to give an overview of the main findings.

The survey shows a positive attitude within all three groups towards increased student influence in higher education governance, regardless of the present level of student influence in the different countries.

Some areas that need special consideration were identified:

- The student representation and participation at national level, in relation to the governments as well as to other national bodies, is not as strong as at institutional level. This is true for formal as well as informal participation.

- At department level student representation is also regulated to a lesser extent and student influence seems to be weaker at this level compared to the institutional and faculty levels.

- The relation between formal provisions for participation and the actual practices at the different levels needs closer examination.

- The role of the student organisations at the different levels, their internal division of powers and organisation, the support they receive from other stakeholders within higher education and the often low participation in the election of student representatives are issues that also need further examination.

- Another finding is that all stakeholders within higher education need to focus on the dissemination of information about the rights of the students, how they can influence the governance of higher education and the results of decisions and discussions relevant to them.

When treating the issue of student participation in the governance of higher education in Europe it becomes clear that a study on the governance of higher education in general, and the participation of all stakeholders, would be an important topic for further study.

Disagreement between representatives of the same country in the cases where two or three groups have responded is a common feature in the survey. This may be because of actual differences within the country, between regions or institutions for higher education. Universities and other higher education institutions may have varying sets of regulations and there may be different rules governing public and private institutions. Higher education is also governed and administered at different administrative levels within a country. Another reason for diverging answers from the respondents may be unclear regulations or a lack of information concerning student representation and participation in the governance of higher education.

There are no obvious differences between the answers from the three groups in the survey in general. None of the groups seem to have a clearly more positive or negative opinion of student participation in the governance of higher education in Europe.

Formal provision for student participation in higher education governance based on national legislation

A narrow majority of respondents state that there are legal or constitutional mechanisms to ensure student representation in higher education governance at the national level. The areas they concern differ, but the most commonly mentioned are laws on the representation of students within national decision making, advisory or evaluation bodies, the status of the national student organisation and rules governing consultation procedures or meetings with the ministry responsible for higher education.

All of the respondents except two reply that student representation and participation is ensured by legal mechanisms at the institutional level (institutional, faculty and/or department levels). All countries that have such legal mechanisms answer that student representation at institution level is ensured by law, and most of them also regulate the participation at the level of the faculty. To regulate student representation at department level is not as common, even if a majority of respondents delivered an affirmative answer to the question.

Most of the countries have minimum legal or constitutional requirements for student representation on the board of the institution, usually expressed as a minimum percentage of the seats and to a lesser extent as a minimum number of seats, or a combination of these two alternatives. The most common percentage interval indicated by the respondents is the 11-20% range, followed by the interval just above (21-30%) and the one just below (1-10%).

The department level seems to be the level where student representation is regulated to a lesser extent. This is also the level where it is most difficult to find student candidates for elective positions and that receives lower indications than other levels concerning student influence.

The students have voting rights in the governance bodies concerned. Only four country representatives (with compatriots disagreeing in three of the cases) in total replied that students do not have the right to vote in the governance bodies where students are represented. A majority of the respondents also reply that the right to vote covers all issues treated by the bodies concerned. Eleven respondents, mainly students, reply that this is not the case. The areas that are not covered by the student right to vote are primarily staff matters and administrative and finance issues.

A majority of the respondents answer that there are requirements for higher education institutions to have a policy on student participation. However, twenty-eight respondents representing twenty countries (in half of the cases compatriots disagree) answered that there are no such requirements. Of these respondents, 40% indicated that there are no such regulations, but that most of the institutions nevertheless do have a policy on student participation.

In most countries political student organisations are legal, even if there are quite a few countries where they are not (42% of the countries represented in the survey). Candidates for elections are in a minority of the cases presented through political student organisations. Nevertheless, political influence on student organisations is an issue that is raised and discussed by many respondents relating to several of the survey questions.

Student representatives are elected directly in a majority of countries represented in the survey. To a lesser extent they are elected indirectly. In the few cases where student representatives are appointed, the student organisations make the appointment. This could perhaps even be considered a kind of indirect election. In a vast majority of the countries surveyed there are also laws or regulations relating to how student representatives should be elected. These regulations mainly state that elections should take place through secret ballot, lay down the minimum requirements for the necessary percentage of the student electorate participating in the elections, and concern who can vote, the number of candidates and the obligation to establish an election commission to monitor the election.

Half of the respondents reply that student evaluation of courses and programmes is required by law or other regulations, while the other half consequently states that this is not the case.

Other provision for student participation in higher education governance

In the majority of the countries surveyed there is regular contact between the government or the ministry responsible for higher education, and student representatives. Some respondents explain that the contacts might not be regular in the sense of weekly or monthly gatherings, but more of a situation-related contact when considered necessary. Very few reply that these contacts are restricted to certain areas within higher education policy. Still there are at least ten countries where such regular contacts do not exist.

A majority of the student representatives state that there is student participation or representation in relation to the national rectors' conferences or other equivalent bodies. The ministry representatives that have answered the question, however, mainly give a negative answer. The academic replies were neither affirmative nor negative.

The question as to whether student representatives or student bodies have regular informal or formal contacts with the national parliamentary assembly receives a narrow majority of affirmative answers from the students and the ministry representatives. The academic representatives have a more positive opinion of the situation.

A majority of the respondents reply that there are other formal and informal procedures to ensure student influence on higher education governance at the national level than those treated in the questionnaire. The most common forms are informal consultations and seminars, student representation in temporary working groups or projects of the ministry, informal contacts between the students and the ministry and the parliament and representation in national councils or committees on higher education and student affairs. However, respondents representing twenty-two countries say that "other formal or informal procedures" do not exist.

A majority, strongest within the student group, reply that there is no division of power between student organisations at national level and at the institutional level concerning higher education governance. In a few countries there is no – or at least no active – national student body. A very large majority, however, affirm that there is regular communication between national and institutional student organisations on governance issues.

Actual practice of student participation

In a large majority of the cases it is in general possible to find enough candidates to occupy all elective positions reserved for students. Only five respondents in total answer negatively. The respondents were also asked to specify if there is any level where there are particular problems in finding candidates to occupy the seats. The levels where in some countries there are problems are primarily faculty and department level. Respondents representing fourteen out of the thirty-six countries in the survey show difficulties on at least one of the levels. In nine of these countries, however, compatriots answering do not agree that there are difficulties.

Candidates for student elections are in a majority of the cases presented through non-political organisations or individually. The least common way of presenting candidates according to this survey is through political student organisations. If all answers are totalled, the largest group answers that candidates are presented only through non-political student organisations regardless of level. The second largest group replies that there is a mixture of all three ways of presenting candidates at different levels. At institutional and faculty level, candidates are mainly presented through non-political student organisations. At the department level, however, a majority of the three groups indicate that candidates are presented individually.

In order to be a candidate in student elections a minimum number of signatures from the student electorate is required on at least one level, mainly institutional and faculty level, in fifteen of the thirty-six countries represented in the survey (some of these having compatriots giving contradictory answers). The age of student representatives is in general between 20 and 27.

The average percentage of students participating in the election of student representatives to university bodies or student organisations varies greatly between countries, regions, institutions and levels of governance. The range most frequently indicated is that between 16-30%, followed by the interval just below (0-15%) and the one just above (31-45%). Only two respondents representing the same country indicate that the percentage is higher than 76%.

In most of the countries protocols and decisions arising from meetings of university governance bodies are public. Respondents representing fifteen countries state that this is not the case. More than half of these do, however, have fellow nationals that do not agree. A majority of the respondents reply that both the university administration and the student organisations take steps to disseminate information about such protocols and decisions. The students, nevertheless, seem to have a lower estimation of the dissemination activities of the university administration than the other two groups.

Student influence appears to be strongest on social and environmental issues at the institutions, at institutional level generally, and on pedagogical issues and educational content issues. The weakest influence is exercised on budget matters and on the criteria for employment of teaching staff and admission of students. There are no large differences between the estimations made by the three different groups. Students seem to consider their influence to be slightly stronger at national level, concerning the institutional level generally, and relating to social and environmental issues at the institutional level compared to the other two groups. The academic representatives estimate student influence on educationally related issues and budget issues to be stronger than the students and ministry officials do.

The strongest levels for student influence seem to be the institutional and faculty levels. Both the students and the ministry representatives answering the question consider these as the levels where influence is strongest. Student influence is also considered to be the lowest at national level by both students and ministries. The academic representatives agree that the faculty level is quite strong, but consider the national level to be just as strong. Student influence is by the academics considered to be the weakest at department level.

A large majority of the respondents (90% of the students, 70% of the ministry representatives and 72% of the academic representatives) consider that student influence on higher education governance should increase. Most of the respondents in all three groups that have answered negatively consider that the student influence on higher education in their country is strong enough as it is today. Nevertheless, some of these respondents say that the actual student influence should increase.

The respondents stating that student influence on higher education governance should increase say that the students have a right to influence decisions and practices since they are the largest group within higher education and the main stakeholders. The students are well informed and their influence enhances the quality of higher education. Students may also be a driving force behind changes. It is also important to enhance democracy within the institutions. Some of the respondents consider there to be a difference between the formal and actual influence of students on higher education. Where the influence is not very strong formally it may still

38

be very strong in practice. The opposite situation may also be true. There are no large differences between the three groups concerning the reasons behind wanting to increase student influence.

Concerning the question of how student influence should increase, all three groups focus on the formal aspects of governance influence such as a higher number of seats reserved for students at all levels, stronger rights to vote and speak within the bodies concerned, and regulated rights to participate in evaluation procedures. Some ministry representatives emphasise that the present legal framework should be applied to a larger extent. All three groups mention the heavy responsibility of the students and student organisations to use the opportunities for influence and to organise themselves accordingly at the different levels. The students say that they need support from other stakeholders and the legal framework in order to be able to increase their participation in and influence on higher education governance. The national level is mentioned as the weakest level for student influence because of a lack of regulation at that level and sometimes no, or weak, national student organisations.

Analysis of the questionnaire on formal provisions for student participation in higher education governance based on national legislation

Legal mechanisms at the national level

Question 2.1 Does your country have legal or constitutional mechanisms to ensure student representation in higher education governance at the national level?

More than half of the countries replying, twenty-two[35] out of the thirty-six countries represented, have at least one group representative answering that legal or constitutional mechanisms to ensure student representation in higher education governance at the national level exist. A majority of the student and the ministry representatives, and 46% of the academic representatives confirm that this is the case.

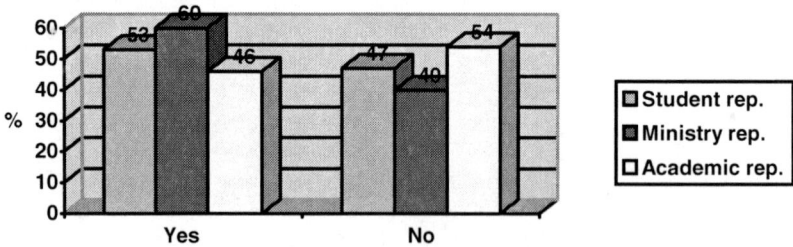

The areas the legal or constitutional mechanisms concern differ, but those most commonly mentioned are:

- laws on the representation of students within a national higher education council or other decision-making, advisory or evaluating bodies relevant to higher education;
- the status of the national student organisation;
- rules governing consultation procedures or meetings with the ministry responsible for higher education.

In twelve of the twenty-five countries with more than one group answering the respondents differ in their reply, but there is no visible pattern in the diverging answers according to the groups the respondents represent. In some cases divergences can be explained by actual differences between regions, communities, between public and private institutions or within binary systems of higher education. In some countries new legislation is also on its way, which may cause divergent answers. The divergence may also be

---

[35] In twelve out of twenty-five countries with more than one representative answering the respondents do not agree. See text.

because of a lack of knowledge of the system or of a common understanding of the situation in a specific country.

In a few cases the divergent answers can also be the result of a misinterpretation of the question. In their comments, some respondents appear to have thought that the question was whether there was a law or another mechanism at the national level to ensure student representation within higher education in general. The question was, however, whether there are legal or constitutional mechanisms to ensure the *representation* of students at the *national* level, in national committees or councils for example.

Some of the countries representing different actors within the higher education community that answered that there are no legal or constitutional mechanisms to ensure student representation at the national level state that even if there might be a lack of regulation at the national level, the participation of students within national bodies is ensured by practice.

Legal mechanisms at the higher education institutions

Question 2.2 Does your country have legal mechanisms to ensure student representation and participation in the governance of higher education institutions?

All of the countries but two that have representatives replying to the questionnaire do have legal mechanisms to ensure student representation and participation in the governance of higher education institutions. The countries that gave a negative reply are geographically small with a limited number of higher education institutions.

Question 2.3 If yes, at what levels of governance within the institution is student representation regulated by law or other means?

The respondents answering Question 2.2 in the affirmative were also asked to indicate at what levels of governance within the institution student representation is regulated by law or other means. All country representatives within all three groups[36] answer that student representation at the institution level is ensured by law, and most institutions also legally regulate participation at faculty level.

---

[36] One student representative in one of the countries with two students replying has a diverging opinion.

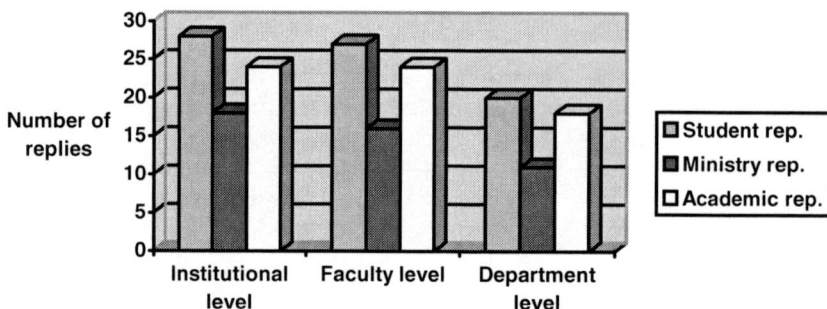

The legal regulation of student representation at department or institute level is not as common, even if the majority of respondents gave an affirmative answer to the question. Some 69%[37] of the students, 61%[38] of the ministry representatives and 75%[39] of the academic representatives indicate that there is legislation concerning student representation at this level.

In ten of the twenty-five countries where several group representatives have answered, the respondents have diverging opinions as to whether student representation is regulated by law on a specific level or not, primarily whether or not there are regulations at department level. No pattern according to group adherence is visible.

Eight country representatives from different groups also indicate other levels of governance where student representation is ensured by law. Examples mentioned were doctoral schools, official advisory bodies, other organisations and committees within the institution such as committees on learning environment, study plans etc. In one of the countries presenting examples, each university has a student vice-rector at the institutional level and each faculty has a student vice-dean at faculty level.

Question 2.4 Is there a minimum legal or constitutional requirement for student representation, for example as a percentage or a certain number of seats that have to be reserved for students within the board of the institution? If yes, what percentage or number?

All country representatives but nine state[40] that they do have minimum legal or constitutional requirements for student representation within the board of the institution. Of the representatives answering "no", two explain the answer as being because such legislation is the responsibility of administrative levels below the national level. This might be the case for several countries and a reason for some representatives not to answer the question at all. In three cases the student representatives have answered "no" where other

---

[37] Twenty out of twenty-nine students answering the question.
[38] Eleven out of eighteen ministry representatives.
[39] Eighteen out of twenty-four academic representatives.
[40] Four students, one ministry representative and four academics, two from the same country.

representatives (ministry in one case and academic in all three cases) of the same country have indicated "yes".

Most commonly, requirements for student participation are stipulated in percentage terms; far less frequently a minimum number of seats are reserved for student representatives. In at least twelve countries a combination of percentage and number is used.

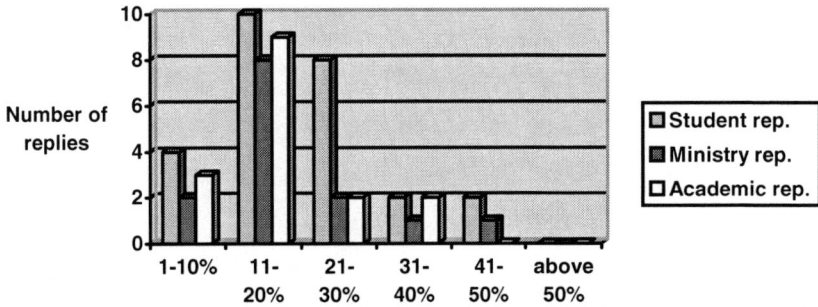

Twenty-three students (representing twenty-one countries) and thirteen representatives from each of the other two groups indicate that there are minimum requirements and that these concern a percentage of seats that have to be reserved for students on the board of the institution.

The most commonly indicated range is that between 11-20%. The 11-20% range has been indicated by 38% of the student, 57% of the ministry and 56% of the academic respondents. The level just above (21-30%) is the second most common, at least according to the students. The academic and ministry groups give a slightly higher number indicating the 1-10% level. A few countries indicate several alternatives. Representatives from ten of the countries do not agree on the level, but in all but one country they have marked the percentage levels next to each other. In six of these cases at least one of the representatives of a country has marked "number" instead of "percentage" as the requirement.

Six students, four ministry officials and nine academics have replied that the requirement concerns the number of seats reserved for students. Not even half of these, however, indicate the total number of seats on the governing board, so it is difficult to draw any conclusions from their answers.

In at least one country the percentage requirement is not a minimum requirement, which appears to be the most frequent, but a maximum requirement. In this particular case, none of the three stakeholders – (professors, other teachers and staff, students) can occupy more than 50% of the seats on the governing body. In another country the student representative cannot be a first- or a final-year student. In yet another country the students on the governing board of the institution have a veto for issues directly concerning students.

Question 2.5 Do the students have the right to vote in the governance bodies concerned?

Only four country representatives in total replied negatively to the question of whether students have the right to vote in the governance bodies concerned. In three of these it is student representatives that have answered "no", while other representatives of the same country in all three cases have given a positive reply. In one case the student's negative reply is explained by this not being a legislative issue at the national level, but on the regional level, which may well be the case in several countries. The fourth "no" answer comes from an academic representative without any compatriots answering. One ministry representative who does not answer the question says that this depends on which body is concerned.

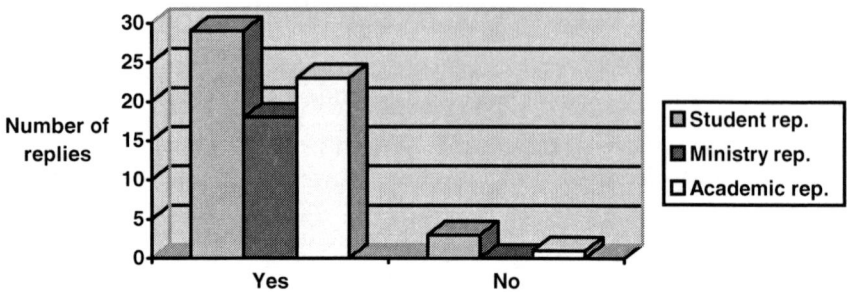

Question 2.5 cont. If yes, does the right to vote cover all issues treated by the bodies concerned?

The majority of respondents give an affirmative answer to this part of the question.

Eight student representatives (two representing the same country), as well as one ministry and two academic representatives, answer "no". These in total represent eight countries. In six of the countries the student "no", however, differs from other answers from the same country. The student representatives answering "no" have in six cases given examples of issues on which students do not have the right to vote. These concern:

- staff matters;
- administrative and finance issues;
- issues related to doctoral degrees and theses (notably when the student representative has not reached that level of study);
- the issue of employability;
- educational processes;
- curricula;
- the recognition of academic degrees.

In one country the right to vote is said to be general at the institutional level, but not within the governing bodies of faculties and departments. The two academic examples of issues on which student representatives do not have the right to vote relate to the filling of vacant academic posts.

Policies on student participation

Question 2.6 Are the higher education institutions required by law/constitution/agreement to have a policy on student participation?

In a majority of the countries in the survey the higher education institutions are required by law, constitution or agreement to have a policy on student participation. However, seventeen respondents, representing twelve countries, have given a negative answer. Eleven respondents, representing nine countries, have chosen the third option: "No, but most of them have".

The majority, fourteen out of twenty-five, of countries from which several different representatives have replied, disagree on this issue. The only visible difference between the groups that could be mentioned is that in three of the cases the academic representative has answered "yes" and the others "no".

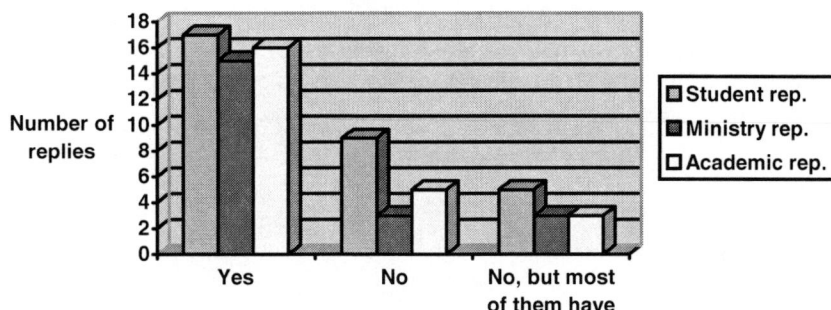

Question 2.7 To your knowledge are there policies within higher education institutions that ensure a stronger student participation in the governance than those required by law?

A majority of the students and the ministry representatives answered this question in the negative, most notably in the ministry group where twelve out of nineteen (63%) answered "no". Eighteen student representatives out of thirty-one answering the question (58%) gave the same reply. In the academic group there was an equal amount of positive and negative answers (twelve-twelve).

There was disagreement on this issue within ten of the twenty-five countries from which several different groups have replied, which is not surprising since the question asks for the personal experience of the respondents.

45

None of the groups seems to have a more (or less) favourable view of the situation than the others.

The examples of a stronger student influence than that required by law include a higher percentage of student representatives in governing bodies, or students themselves being organised in a different way in order to have a stronger influence on the governance of the institution. One country representative also mentions the veto right of students on the boards of the institutions of the country in question.

Becoming a student representative

Question 2.8 Are political student organisations at the higher education institutions legal?

A majority within all three groups have replied that political student organisations at the higher education institutions are legal. There are, however, quite a few countries where this is not the case as representatives of fifteen out of the total of thirty-six countries (42%) represented in the survey gave a negative answer. In two countries there is disagreement on this issue, but no pattern that can be tracked to the groups they represent. With two exceptions, the countries that have replied in the negative are located in eastern or South-east Europe.

The term "political" was not defined in the questionnaire, but according to the answers it seems to have been interpreted as party political, which also was the intention in the survey.

All the countries represented in the survey

Number of replies

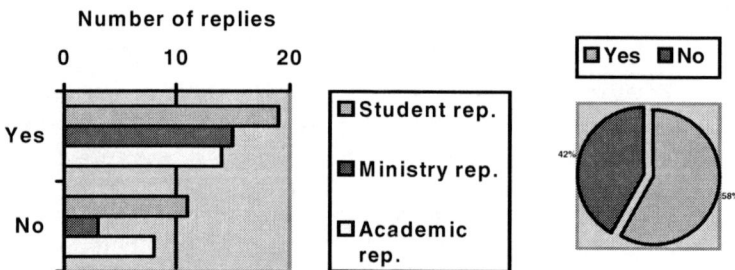

46

Question 2.9 How do you become a student representative?

On the issue of how one becomes a student representative a large majority[41] of the total amount of respondents answered that this is done through direct election. Many[42] also answered that indirect elections are used. Eight students, five ministry officials and four academics have stated that both ways are possible.

Eight respondents from five countries replied that student representatives are appointed, in most cases by the student unions at different levels. In one case, student representatives are said to be appointed by the departments and in another by the university or faculty board. In the latter case, however, a legal change is on its way. In one country, students are sometimes nominated by the student unions, but formally appointed by the government if representation within a national body is involved.

Question 2.10 Are there laws or regulations concerning how student representatives should be elected?

In a vast majority of the countries replying to the questionnaire there are laws and regulations concerning how student representatives should be elected.

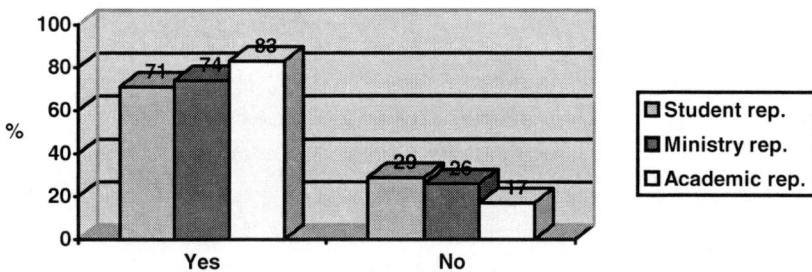

These regulations mainly state that, out of the alternative choice of answers given in the questionnaire, student representatives should be elected by secret ballot. In many countries a minimum percentage of the student electorate participating in the election is required and for some both are obligatory. Other laws and regulations added by the respondents relate to who can vote, the number of candidates, the requirement of an election commission or a monitoring forum, timetables, deadlines, the campaign, etc. These regulations may differ between higher education institutions and local student unions. In one country the local student union statutes have to be approved by the board of the institutions, which is seen as a guarantee against non-democratic statutes. In another country there has to be a proportional representation of all the political organisations active within the student unions.

---

[41] 73% of the students, 72% of the ministry officials and 74% of the academics.
[42] 43% of the students, 44% of the ministry officials and 35% of the academics.

About half of the countries with several respondents, thirteen out of twenty-five, have not reached an agreement on whether there are laws and regulations concerning how student representatives should be elected. This confusion may primarily be because of the uncertainty as to whether the respondents had national or local regulations in mind or to differences between parts of the country.

Student evaluation of courses and programmes

Question 2.11 Are student evaluations of courses and programmes required by law or other regulations?

More than half of the total amount of respondents, 53%, state that student evaluation of courses and programmes is not required by law or other regulations.

Among the students sixteen answer "yes" and sixteen "no" (one respondent gives both replies). Within the ministry group seven countries answer "yes" and thirteen "no". In the academic group thirteen reply "yes" and eleven "no".

The relatively large number of negative answers among the ministry representatives may indicate that the regulations are not normally decided at national level, but at regional or institutional level. This is also found in some of the statements made and might explain the fact that respondents from the same country sometimes differ in their answers. The regulations may not be legally binding.

Respondents from one country indicate that there are regulations concerning student evaluations of courses and programmes, but that these evaluations are not carried out in practice. The opposite is also true since another country states that students and graduates are consulted during external evaluations/peer reviews of programmes. Respondents from yet another country say that evaluations of courses and programmes are not regulated, but on the other hand student evaluations of teachers are required by law.

Analysis of the questionnaire on other provisions for student participation in higher education governance

Contacts at national level

Question 3.1 Are there regular contacts between the government or the ministry responsible for higher education and student representatives, for example within a national forum on the Bologna Process?

A majority of the respondents reply that there are regular contacts between the government or the ministry responsible for higher education and student representatives, for example within a national forum on the Bologna Process. The student representatives give the strongest affirmative answer, nineteen students representing seventeen countries answer "yes", while twelve students representing eleven countries answer "no" to the question.

The answers from the ministries have a slight majority answering "yes" (twelve-ten) and academic representatives from thirteen countries confirm that there are regular contacts and nine that there are not.

Number of replies   **Percentage within each group**

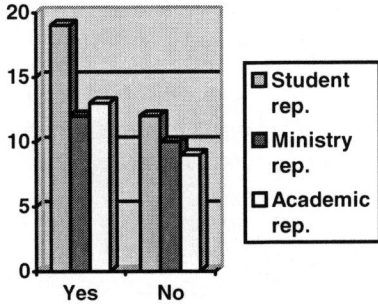

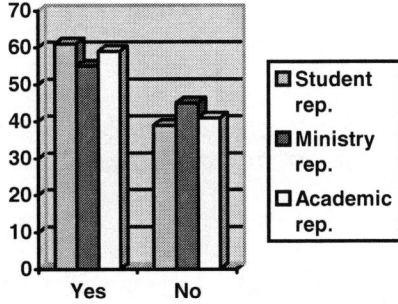

Respondents from some countries explain that the contacts might not be regular in the sense of weekly or monthly gatherings, but more of a situation-related contact when considered necessary.

Countries from eastern or South-east Europe dominate the group of countries answering "no", while no Nordic countries appear in the same category.

Another way to present the result is to say that at least one representative from twenty-six of the thirty-six countries answering the question gave a positive answer, but answers from representatives of different groups from the same country diverge in twelve of the countries. Where the answers from the same country differ, no differences according to the group to which the respondents belong can be seen.

Among the countries giving an affirmative reply to the first part of Question 3.1 only six (four ministry and two academic) state that these contacts are restricted to certain areas. Where the contacts are restricted the areas of contact concern specific student-related issues such as study loans/financing, housing etc., but in two cases the contact is claimed to be restricted to questions such as those relating to the Bologna Process and the quality of study programmes.

Question 3.2 Is there student participation or representation in relation to the national rectors' conferences or other equivalent bodies?

A majority of the student representatives (seventeen answers representing seventeen countries) state that there is student participation or representation in relation to the national rectors' conferences or other

49

equivalent bodies. Thirteen student representatives from twelve countries answered "no" to the same question. The ministry replies show only five affirmative answers and twelve negative. The academic replies show eleven "yes" and thirteen "no".

The difference between the replies of the students and the ministries might arise from the fact that ministries are not involved when students and rectors' conferences meet. Still, a slight majority of the academic representatives also answer negatively, which is harder to explain. Discrepancies in the answers from the same country (in twelve cases) may be because of sectoral or regional/local differences. In one case the participation of students is said to have been introduced very recently, which may also provide an explanation for the diverging answers.

Question 3.3 Do student representatives or student bodies have regular informal or formal contact with the national parliamentary assembly?

This question receives a majority of affirmative answers from all three groups; a narrow majority in the case of the students and the ministries. Sixteen students, eleven ministry officials and fifteen academics answer "yes". Fifteen students give a negative answer as compared to nine ministry officials and six academics. Not many representatives from the same country disagree on this issue.

Question 3.4 Are there any other formal or informal procedures to ensure student influence on higher education governance at national level?

The last question in this section concerns any other formal or informal procedures, besides the ones discussed previously, to ensure student influence on higher education governance at national level. A majority of the respondents reply that their countries have other procedures.

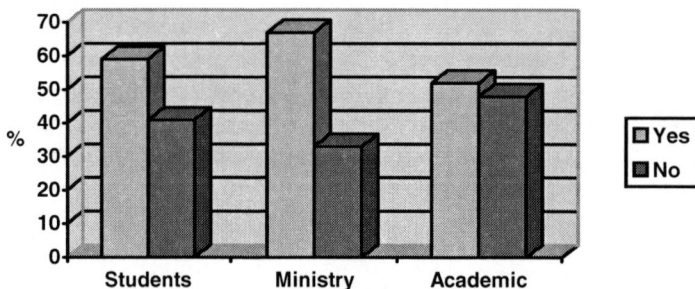

Forty-five respondents representing twenty-four countries answer "yes" and thirty-one respondents representing twenty-two countries answer "no". Respondents from eleven countries disagree on the issue and in six of these the students differ from the other respondents by making a more positive estimation of the situation.

Many respondents give examples of how these formal or informal procedures are carried out. The most common forms of procedure seem to be through:

- informal consultations and seminars;
- representation on non-permanent working groups or projects of the ministry;
- informal contacts with ministry officials;
- written or oral contact with members of parliament;
- representation in national councils, agencies or committees in charge of student affairs, quality assurance etc.

Individual representatives mention collective demonstrations by the students and contacts between students and employer organisations or trade unions at the national level. In two countries, student unions are said to be a part of the political system or students are members of parliament, thus maintaining contact at the national level.

Student organisations at national and institutional level

Question 3.5 Is there a division of powers between student organisations at national level and at the institutional level concerning higher education governance?

A majority of the respondents state that there is no division of powers between student organisations at national level and at the institutional level concerning higher education governance.

Among the student representatives eleven countries answer "yes" and sixteen "no".[43]

Among the ministry representatives seven countries answer "yes" and thirteen "no".

Among the academic representatives ten countries answer "yes" and ten "no".

In the second part of Question 3.5 the respondents were encouraged to describe the division of powers, if there was such a division. Most of the examples concern a system where the local student unions are autonomous and responsible for the participation and representation at the local level. The local student unions elect or appoint members to a national student union that is responsible for issues of common concern at national level, in relation to the government etc. There might also be an intermediate regional union elected by the local unions. One country explains that the division of powers is carried out in practice, but not by statute.

---

[43] The representatives from one of the countries with several student replies do not agree on this issue.

In a few countries, however, there is no – or at least not an active – national student body.

In eleven of the twenty-five countries from which several representatives have answered the respondents do not agree, or are not familiar with,the fact that there is a division of power between the local and national level of student organisations.

Question 3.6 Is there regular communication between national and institutional student organisations on governance issues?

A very large majority of the respondents affirm that there is regular communication between national and institutional student organisations on governance issues. Twenty-seven of the student representatives belong to this group, while four have replied negatively. Negative answers were received from four representatives in the academic as well as the ministry group, even though the countries are not the same in any of the groups. Twelve ministry officials and thirteen academics answered "yes".

The communication is carried out through regular meetings and assemblies at national level, conferences on a specific topic, information activities on behalf of the national student unions, such as newsletters and Internet sites, and contact through telephone, e-mail etc. In one country, a minimum of four meetings per year between the president of the national student union and the presidents of the local student unions is required by law. Another country describes how proposals from the government are always transmitted to the local student unions for consultation, and yet another country offers training to the local unions on important issues.

Analysis of the questionnaire on actual practice of student participation

Candidates for elective positions

Question 4.1 If there are legal provisions for student participation is it – in general – possible to find enough candidates to occupy all elective positions reserved for students?

Only five respondents in total answer negatively, and in four of these cases compatriots answering the question did not agree.

Comments on this particular question by student representatives show that student bodies within faculties, programmes and subjects are important in motivating the students to act as representatives of the student body. The role of the institution in motivating the students is also important. The same people do, however, show up as representatives in different contexts and the student unions are often dependent on a few very active students. This indicates a problem regarding how the student body in general is represented and the democratic base of the elected students.

One ministry representative states that the financial support from the government to the national student union and from the institutions to the student representatives at the local level may be an important factor in motivating students to run for representative posts. Two respondents, one ministry and one academic representative, also argue that the students are motivated because active participation provides a good experience in preparation for a future political or other career.

Question 4.2. Is there any level where there are particular problems in finding candidates to occupy the seats reserved for students?

This question asks the respondents to specify this issue a bit further and indicate if there is any level where there are particular problems to find candidates to occupy the seats reserved for students.

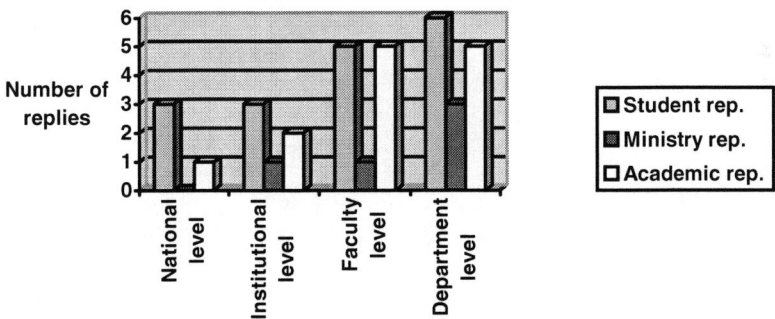

Out of thirty-one students answering the question representatives of nine countries (32% of the representatives) indicate a certain degree of difficulty at different levels, mainly faculty (four countries) and department (six countries) level. At the national and institutional level students representing three countries indicate problems.

Out of sixteen ministry representatives answering the question, four countries (25%) indicate some problems, mainly at the department level as well.

Out of twenty-one academic representatives answering the question, seven (33%) demonstrate the difficulties, even though only one country has problems at national level and two at institutional level. One academic country representative not indicating problems at any particular level does, however, state that there are sometimes problems with students not being active enough in their positions.

Respondents representing fourteen out of the total thirty-six countries indicate difficulties. In nine of these cases compatriots answering do not agree; four countries do not have compatriots answering. The Nordic countries indicate slightly greater difficulties in finding candidates to occupy the seats reserved for students than the other countries do.

Presentation in elections

Question 4.3 How are candidates for student representatives in your country normally presented in the elections at the different levels?

In the elections at different levels, candidates for student representatives are normally presented through non-political student organisations or individually. In a number of countries students are also presented through the third option given in the question – political student organisations.

If we add all of the answers from the respondents, the largest group (twenty-two respondents representing sixteen countries) answers that candidates are presented *only* through non-political student organisations regardless of level.

The second largest group, sixteen respondents (representing ten countries), replies that there is a mixture of all three ways of presenting candidates at different levels. All Nordic countries belong to this group.

The third largest group, fourteen respondents (representing ten countries), is the one where candidates are presented only as individuals, regardless of level. Twelve respondents, representing ten countries, show a mixture of presentation through non-political organisations and individually.

The least frequent model is where the candidates present themselves only through political student organisations, six respondents representing four countries belong to this group.

In half of the countries from which several representatives have replied, the respondents do not agree on which of the abovementioned groups they belong to, which makes it difficult to draw any conclusions from the result above.

Number of replies[44]

Institutional level

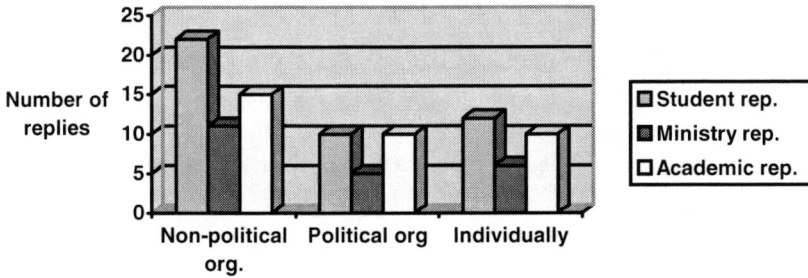

Faculty level

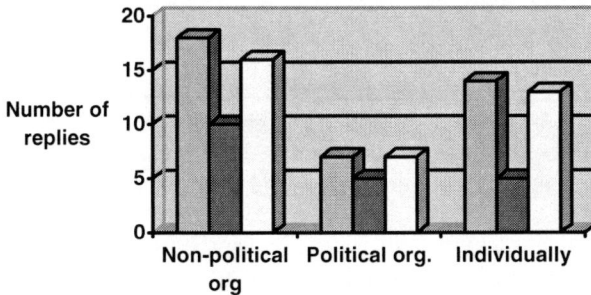

At the institutional level a majority of the respondents state that the candidates are presented through non-political student organisations. Among the student respondents twenty-two indicate non-political student organisations, ten political student organisations and twelve individually. Among the ministry representatives the corresponding numbers are eleven, five, six and the academic representatives fifteen, ten, ten.

With slight differences, the same pattern was shown for the faculty level with a tendency towards a stronger emphasis on individually proposed candidates and not as many for the alternative option for "political student organisations".

---

[44] It is theoretically possible for a respondent to choose all of the options given.

Department level

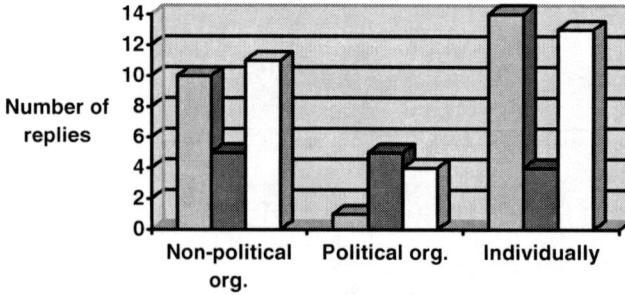

At the department/institute level only one student representative has indicated that students are presented through political student organisations together with five of the ministry and four of the academic representatives. There is a total majority of representatives of the three groups that at the department level tick "individually" as the main way of presenting candidates, but the ministry replies differ. However, the department level seems to be the level with which the respondents are least familiar, or that to a lesser extent fits the alternatives given in the questionnaire, since there are fewer replies at this level in total.[45] This seems to especially be the case of the ministries as only ten ministry representatives answered at the department level.

The ministry representatives seem less inclined to indicate the "individual" option than the other two groups for any of the levels.

Question 4.4 Is a minimum number of signatures from the student electorate required?

In fifteen of the thirty-six countries represented by one or several respondents a minimum number of signatures from the student electorate is required on at least one level (mainly institutional and faculty level), in order to be a candidate in student elections. Taking account of the answers in all of the groups, only six countries require a minimum number of signatures at national level and five at department level. In both categories three country representatives disagree. In two of these cases, academic representatives state that signatures are needed at the level indicated, while the students do not.

Apparently the institutional and faculty levels are more strictly regulated, or have a stricter practice known to the country representatives, than the other two levels, since the national and the department level get the least amount of indications in the questionnaires.

In only a very few countries respondents disagree on whether signatures are needed. There are, however, a few more disagreements concerning at what level these are needed. Six out of twenty-one ministry representatives chose not to answer this question.

---

[45] 101 indications in total at institutional level, 95 at faculty level and 67 at department level.

Question 4.5 What is, in general, the age of the student representatives?

The age of the student representatives is in general between 20 and 27. The respondents were asked to indicate a maximum of two alternatives and a majority in all three groups chose the 20-23 years option. Only three representatives chose "under 20" as their only alternative, but the compatriots of one of these respondents do not agree with this answer. According to the answers the student representatives seem to be slightly younger in eastern and southern Europe and older in northern Europe. No representative, however, has indicated the two last age brackets: 28-31 years and over 32 years.

Question 4.6 What is normally the percentage of students participating in the election of student representatives to university bodies or student organisations?

The percentage of students participating in the election of student representatives to university bodies or student organisations varies greatly between countries, regions, institutions and levels of governance. The most frequent answer to the question: what is the usual percentage, is the range from 16-30%, followed by 0-15% and 31-45%. Only two representatives (from the same country) indicate that the percentage is more than 76% and not many indicate a figure higher than 45%. [46] Sixteen respondents, representing ten countries, respond that the percentage is normally 15% or lower. Among these appear some of the northernmost and some of the southernmost countries of Europe.

The students and the ministry representatives generally have a lower estimation of the percentage participating in the elections than the academic representatives. Quite a few, eight out of twenty-one, ministry representatives did not respond to the question.

---

[46] A total of eleven respondents representing nine countries.

Percentage per group[47]

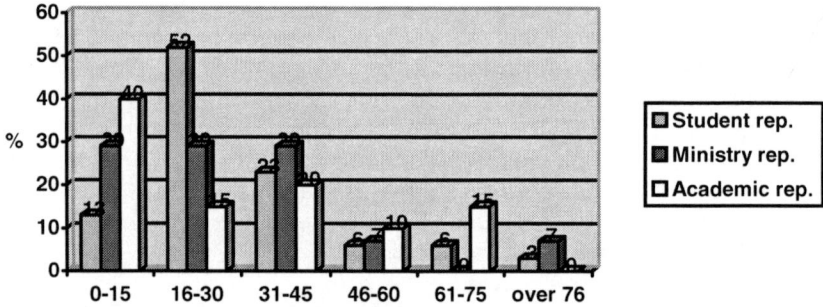

Dissemination of information

Question 4.7 Are protocols and decisions from meetings of university governance bodies at different levels made public?

A large majority in all three groups has answered "yes" to this. question.

Seventeen respondents, representing a total of fifteen countries, state that this is not the case. More than half of these do, however, have compatriots that do not agree with their answer. One of the respondents with compatriots who disagree explains that the rules concerning which decisions or protocols are made public depend on whether the institution is public or private. Another country representative states that the answer to the question differs according to the category of decision or protocols. These two representatives therefore answered both "yes" and "no" to the question.

Percentage per group answering

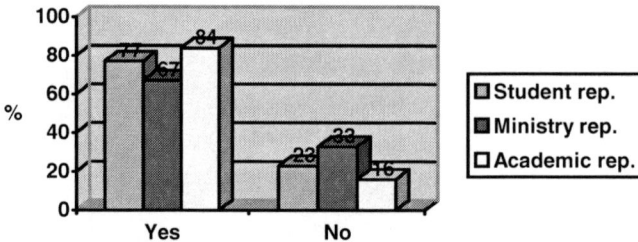

Question 4.8 Does the university administration take steps to disseminate information about such documents and decisions?

A large majority of the respondents answer affirmatively. [48] Six student representatives, representing the same number of countries, say that the

---

[47] Student representatives answering the question: thirty-one (one representative indicating several alternatives). Ministry representatives answering the question: thirteen. Academic representatives answering the question: twenty.

administration does not disseminate this information, but in the cases where those have compatriots answering, these do not agree. Three student representatives have added a third category: "not always". The students seem to have a lower estimation of the dissemination of information from the university administration than the other two groups. Only two academic and two ministry representatives answer "no", or in one case "not always".

Question 4.9 Do student organisations take steps to disseminate information about such documents and decisions?

Only three student representatives declare that student organisations do not take such steps, along with one within each of the ministry and academic categories. Two ministry and two academic representatives, but no students, have added and ticked the category "not always".

The academic representatives seemed to have a slightly higher estimation of the dissemination activities of the university administrations than the students, but in the case of the students' activities the appraisal is similar.

Estimation of influence

Question 4.10 In your opinion how strong is the level of student influence on higher education?

The respondents were asked to estimate the level of student influence on higher education within a number of given alternatives by indicating a number from 1 to 5. Number 1 indicates the influence as very weak and number 5 as very strong.

As mentioned above, the number of respondents and country representatives within the three categories varies. Thirty-one student organisations (representing 28 countries), twenty-one ministry and twenty-four academic representatives (representing the same number of countries) responded to the question. They represent a total of thirty-six countries. Not all of them, however, have graded all of the alternatives below.

Because of the varying numbers of respondents within each group and each alternative, the analysis is based on where the emphasis is put within each group and not the comparison of the exact number of estimations within each alternative. The number of replies for each alternative is indicated in the footnotes.

---

[48] Fourteen out of twenty-three students, ten out of twelve ministry officials and eighteen out of twenty academic representatives.

At national level [49]

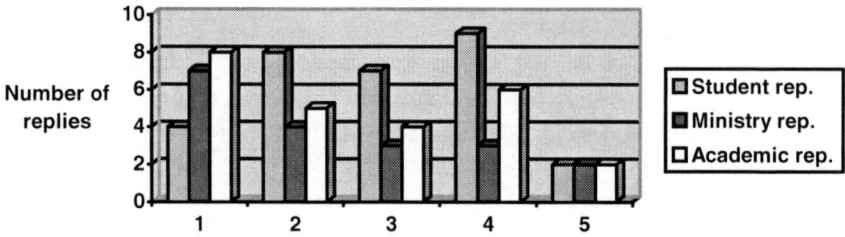

The student organisations seem to consider the student influence at national level to be quite strong, while the the ministry representatives do not. The academic group is more divergent in its answers, but gives an appraisal resembling the ministry rather than the student opinion.

At institutional level generally [50]

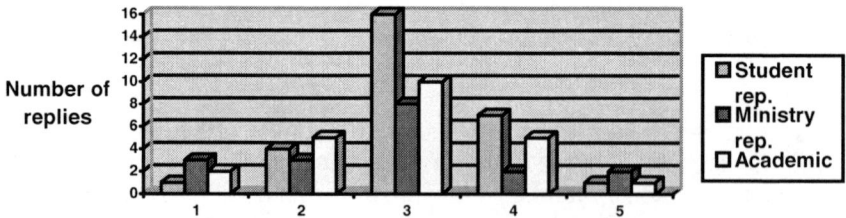

Within this alternative similar estimations have been made within all three groups. They all focus on the middle of the scale, the level of influence being considered neither very weak nor very strong.

---

[49] Thirty student replies, nineteen ministry replies and twenty-five academic replies (one of the latter ticking two options).

[50] Twenty-nine student replies, eighteen ministry replies and twenty-three academic replies.

Institutional governance[51]

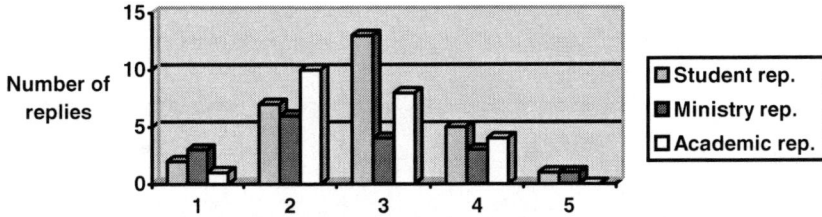

The appraisal of student influence on institutional governance is slightly weaker for all three groups compared to influence at the institutional level generally. The ministry representatives and academic representatives make a somewhat lower estimation of student influence than the students themselves. No academic representative and only one student and one ministry representative estimated the influence of students on institutional governance to be very strong.

Budget matters[52]

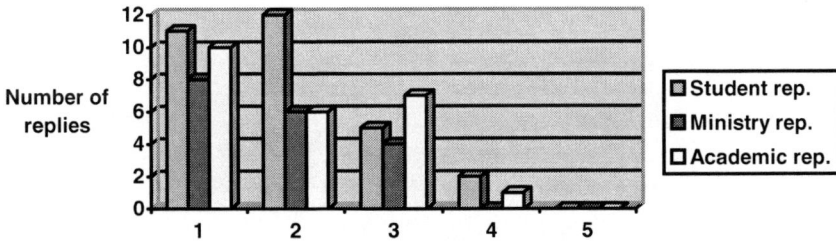

Student influence on budget matters within higher education governance is considered weak by all three groups, with a slightly higher appraisal of the situation by the academic representatives compared to the other groups. None of the groups considers student influence on budget issues to be very strong.

---

[51] Twenty-eight student replies, seventeen ministry replies and twenty-three academic replies.
[52] Thirty student replies, eighteen ministry replies and twenty-four academic replies (one of the latter ticking two alternatives).

Pedagogical issues[53]

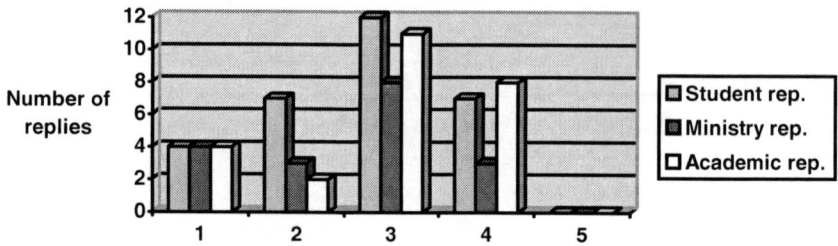

The academic representatives have the most positive view of student influence on pedagogical issues, looking at the histogram and where this group has put its emphasis.. However, none of the representatives of the different groups estimate the influence to be very strong.

Educational content issues[54]

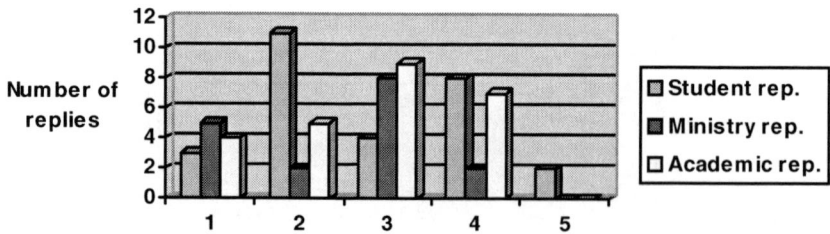

The estimation of the ministry and academic representatives resembles that within the pedagogical issues category, while the students are more negative. Once again the academics give a slightly higher estimation of student influence than the students do. The students, however, take a somewhat divergent position on this issue, but a more negative one compared to the alternative option of "pedagogical issues".

---

[53] Thirty student replies, eighteen ministry replies and twenty-five academic replies (one of the latter ticking two alternatives).
[54] Twenty-eight student replies, seventeen ministry replies and twenty-five academic replies (one of the latter ticking two alternatives).

Criteria for the employment of teaching staff[55]

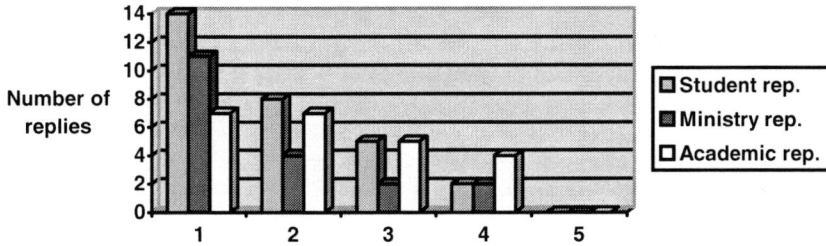

Number of replies

☐ Student rep.
■ Ministry rep.
☐ Academic rep.

Criteria for the admission of students[56]

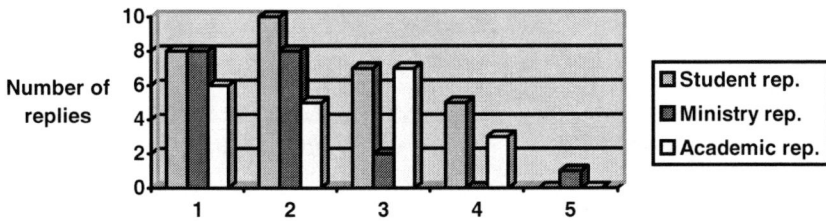

Number of replies

☐ Student rep.
■ Ministry rep.
☐ Academic rep.

Student influence on the criteria for the employment of teaching staff is considered weak by all three groups. Their influence on the criteria for the admission of students is estimated to be slightly stronger. Still, the emphasis of all three groups remains in the lower half of the histogram.

Social and environmental issues at the institution[57]

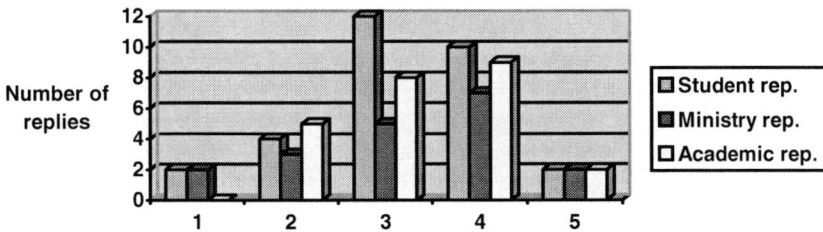

Number of replies

☐ Student rep.
■ Ministry rep.
☐ Academic rep.

This is the area where student influence is considered to be the strongest by all three groups of respondents. However, student influence on social and environmental issues is not the main focus of this survey.

---

[55] Twenty-nine student replies, nineteen ministry replies and twenty-three academic replies.
[56] Thirty student replies, nineteen ministry replies and twenty-two academic replies.
[57] Thirty student replies, nineteen ministry replies and twenty-four academic replies.

The options attracting the strongest degree of student influence seem to be on social and environmental issues at the institutions, at the institutional level generally, on pedagogical issues, and on educational content issues. The weakest influence is exercised on budget matters and on the criteria for the employment of teaching staff and admission of students. Influence at the national level and on institutional governance occupy the middle positions. The institutional governance option receives the lowest number of responses, which may indicate that this particular alternative was more difficult to estimate than the others.

There are no large differences between the estimations made by the three different groups. Students seem to consider their influence to be slightly stronger at the national level, at the institutional level generally, and on social and environmental issues at their institutions compared to the other two groups. The academic representatives estimate that student influence on educationally related issues and budget issues is stronger than the students and ministry officials estimate.

If the answers from the different groups within the twenty-five countries where this can be done are compared, a varying scenario emerges. In one country the groups have given the exact same answers and in another country this is also true for all alternatives but one. Both of these countries have two groups replying.

In four countries the answers follow each other closely (two groups and three groups answering in two cases respectively). In six countries the groups follow each other quite closely (four countries with two groups answering and two countries with three groups answering).

In six countries the answers diverge (three with two groups answering and three with three groups). In yet another six countries the answers diverge largely (two countries with two groups answering and four countries with three groups).

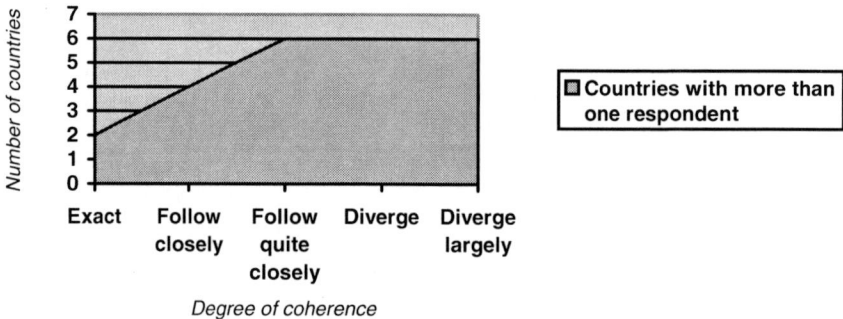

Degree of coherence

There is a quite natural tendency that countries with two groups answering deliver replies that follow each other more closely than countries with three groups. This is, as can be seen above, not the whole explanation.

Among the countries with diverging answers it is not possible to determine which of the groups makes the most positive estimations. There is no discernable geographical pattern concerning which of these countries take a more or less diverging position.

Question 4.11 At which level of governance do you consider students to have the strongest influence? (1 = strongest influence, 2 = second strongest influence etc.)

The respondents were given five options and asked to make their appraisal. Number 1 indicates the level at which students are estimated to have the strongest influence, number 2 indicates the level where they have the second strongest influence etc. Some countries interpreted the instructions in a different manner and indicated only levels 1 and 2, or marked all the levels below level 1 with the number 2. Nevertheless, the appraisals made do give an indication of the level of student influence on higher education governance at different administrative levels.

The numbers have been reversed in the charts in order not to confuse the reader by the value of the numbers compared to the previous question. A high number to the right indicates strong influence.

National level[58]

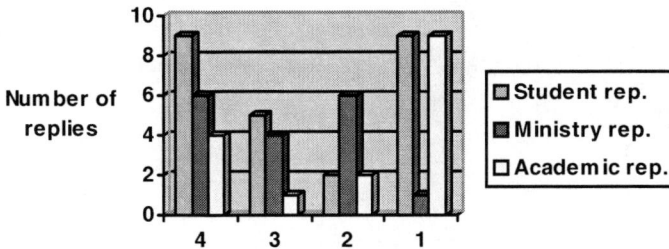

Medium level student representatives: 2.56
Medium level ministry representatives: 2.80
Medium level academic representatives: 2.00
(the lowest number indicating the highest level of influence)

---

[58] Twenty-five student replies, seventeen ministry replies and sixteen academic replies.

Institutional level[59]

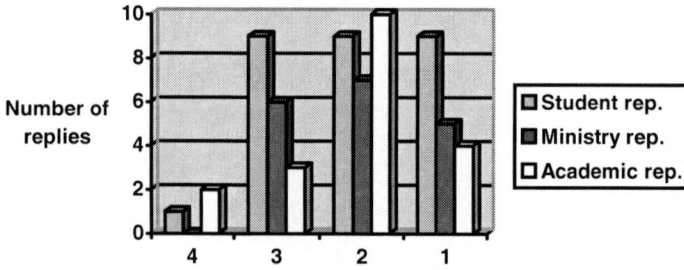

Medium level student representatives: 2.07
Medium level ministry representatives: 2.06
Medium level academic representatives: 2.16
(the lowest number indicating the highest level of influence)

Faculty level[60]

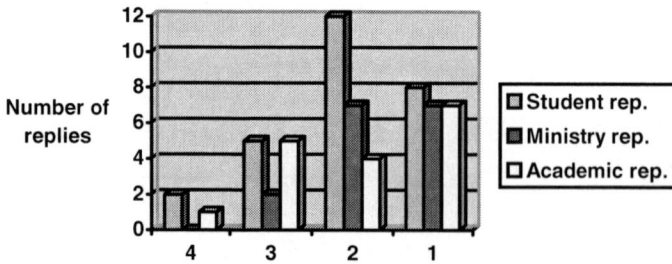

Medium level student representatives: 2.04
Medium level ministry representatives: 1.69
Medium level academic representatives: 2.00
(the lowest number indicating the highest level of influence)

---

[59] Twenty-eight student replies, eighteen ministry replies and nineteen academic replies.
[60] Twenty-seven student replies, sixteen ministry replies and seventeen academic replies.

Department/institute level[61]

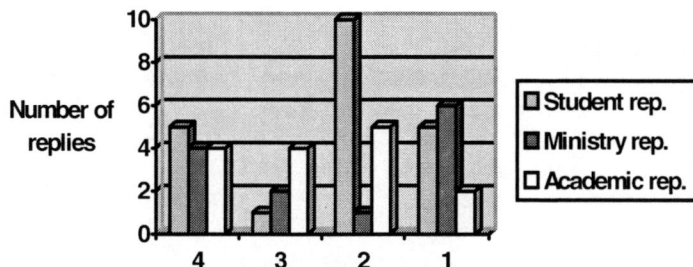

Medium level student representatives: 2.29
Medium level ministry representatives: 2.31
Medium level academic representatives: 3.00
(the lowest number indicating the highest level of influence)

Both the students and the ministry representatives answering the question consider the faculty and the institutional levels to be those at which students have the strongest influence on higher education governance. The national level receives the highest medium number – and is therefore the level where the student influence is estimated to be the lowest – by both the students and the ministry representatives.

The academic representatives estimate that the students have the strongest influence on national and faculty levels of higher education governance and lowest on the department level.

However, the results relating to department level are complicated and it is difficult to draw any conclusions from them since the number of representatives who ranked student influence on this level is lower than those who ranked it at the higher levels. The department level as the weakest or least considered level appears to be a tendency throughout the survey.

Most of the countries from which several different representatives have responded show some kind of coherence, at least concerning which level they consider to have the strongest influence. Of these twenty-five countries, eight show greater divergences.

There was also an opportunity to indicate other levels of governance that were considered relevant. One student representative added the European level and ranked student influence to be weaker on that level than at any of the other levels.

Two ministry representatives added other levels. One of them related to institutional learning environment committees; this was estimated to be the strongest level of student influence. The other ministry representative added social and environmental issues in general and considered that these issues

---

[61] Twenty-one student replies, thirteen ministry replies and fifteen academic replies.

have the weakest student influence, which is not inconsistent with the answers to Question 4.10.

The only academic representative that indicated other levels of governance than the ones given in the questionnaire, ranked programme committees to be the strongest level of influence for the students.

Future developments

Question 4.12 In your opinion, should the student influence in higher education governance increase? If yes, why? How? If no, why not?

The last question was whether the respondents thought that student influence on higher education governance should increase or not.

Negative answers and the reasoning behind them

Student representatives

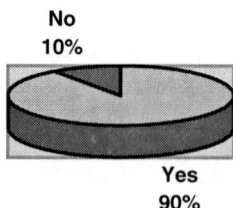

No
10%

Yes
90%

Among the student respondents the "no" answers were very few. Only three (10% of the total amount of student answers to the question) marked this alternative and one of them nevertheless estimates that more legislation is necessary. The two others consider student influence to be strong enough at all levels. One of them, however, emphasises that students participating in the governance of higher education need a better knowledge about higher education governance issues.

Ministry representatives

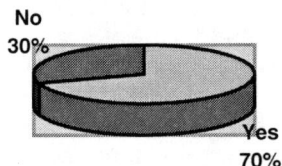

No
30%

Yes
70%

Six of the ministry representatives (30% of the total amount of ministry answers to the question) gave a negative response to the question. One of these has not commented on the answer. The others consider student influence to be strong enough as it is, comparable to the influence on higher education governance of other groups in the higher education community. One representative explains that the students are represented at all levels and that increased formal student participation within higher education governance would be difficult to formalise. Actual influence would, however, be welcomed through a better use of present legislation. Another ministry representative states that students seem to be satisfied with their level of influence. They consider their influence to be dependent on their own activities.

One ministry representative explains the "no" answer by stating that there is a strong political influence on student organisations that prevents them from having independent views on educational issues. S/he claims that students are not very active in the bodies where they are represented if the questions do not have a "significant political relevance".

Academic representatives

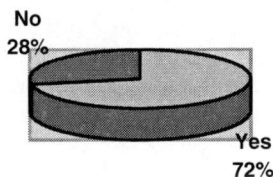

No
28%

Yes
72%

Among the academic representatives, seven (28% of the total amount of academic answers to the question) have responded "no". These consider that students and their views are well represented at the different levels and in the bodies related to the matters that concern them. One respondent states that the informal influence at his/her particular institution is much stronger than the formal influence. Another academic respondent asks if

69

student influence should increase within teaching and learning issues and perhaps decrease related to other issues.

Within the group that answers "no" because they believe that student participation is "strong enough as it is", the Nordic countries are more frequently represented than other geographical areas. This is also to some extent confirmed in the answers to the questionnaire in general.

When comparing the countries from which several group representatives have answered, the student in only one country answered that the student influence should not increase when the other two representatives have said "yes". The opposite, when the ministry and/or the academic representative has answered "no" and the student "yes" is valid for nine countries. In only one country do both representatives agree that student influence on higher education governance should not increase. This is because it is considered strong enough as it is. This is also the country where the two representatives have given exactly the same estimations in Question 4.10.

Affirmative answers and the reasoning behind them

Students: why?

The students replying that their influence on higher education governance should increase in most cases emphasise that students have a right to influence decisions that concern them both directly and indirectly. Their influence is needed to enhance the democracy and the quality of the different parts of the higher education system. The students are the largest group within the higher education community and possess valuable information about the education and the situation of the students. They also have a primary interest in the best possible education. Present problems raised by the student representatives are that students are not considered to be equal partners within the community and are sometimes confronted with a conservative mentality. Some representatives also emphasise the large difference in influence between institutions and some, primarily representatives from South-east Europe, point to a very limited student influence on higher education today. One representative states that there is sometimes a difference between the formal and the actual influence of students and that there are no sanctions available if institutions break laws and regulations concerning student participation.

Students: how?

The students mainly consider that their influence and participation should be increased by having more seats on governing bodies at an increased number of levels, and through stronger laws supporting student participation at all levels. The right to vote and to speak in the different bodies should also be enhanced, as well as student influence on budget matters and educational content issues. Three countries mention the national level as being the main level for enhancing influence. Some student representatives stress that the responsibility of the students and student organisations to participate must be emphasised and encouraged. Conditions for integrating governance participation with other activities or regulations need to be secured. Some argue that students should be paid for their work as representatives. Other ways of increasing influence mentioned by single country representatives are to increase the transparency of the governance procedures, to increase the opportunity for students to influence the agenda-setting of governing bodies, and the creation of a formal national education board with student representation.

Ministry: why?

Several of the ministry representatives answering affirmatively to the question explain their answer by stating that an increased level of student influence and treating students as partners in higher education is needed to enhance the quality and effectiveness of the higher education system. Students are primary actors within higher education. Some of the respondents see students as more reform-minded than other groups and they could be a driving force behind necessary changes within institutions. Several countries mention that the actual influence of students on higher education governance is lower than the level of formal participation and one ministry representative says that the level of student influence is currently very low. Two countries emphasise the need for student influence on labour market-related issues. Another is concerned by the lack of appropriate structures for enhancing student participation and influence within the student organisations.

Ministry: how?

The ministry answers on this issue are very varied. Two country representatives argue that the students themselves need to be more active and effective in the way they organise their participation. They suggest that students should focus on the issues that they consider most important and the whole body of students needs to have a better knowledge of their rights and obligations. Two other countries state that the present legislation might not be in need of reform, but the different levels need to make a better use of the existing legal framework. Other suggestions include that students should be represented in all the bodies and committees at institutional level and participate in the evaluation of their studies including the issue of the relevance of these on the labour market. Students should be better represented at the international level and in the Bologna Process. One ministry representative also proposes more frequent consultations and discussions with the students on higher education issues, and another suggests the creation of political student organisations.

Academic: why?

Within the academic group several of the respondents are of the opinion that students are well informed and give valuable feedback to the higher education institutions on different issues, which increases the quality of the education and the governance of the institutions. Two representatives considered the students to be the main stakeholders of the institutions and therefore it is crucial to have their opinion. The students can also be important partners to enforce necessary changes, for example reforms as a consequence of the Bologna Process. Two academic representatives emphasise the role of students in bringing in new ideas and the importance of their often unbiased approach to challenges. Student involvement is also considered important in order to enhance democracy within the institutions.

Academic: how?

The suggestions from the academic representatives are not very coherent, but emphasis is given to strengthening the legal basis for participation at the different levels, increasing the percentage of seats reserved for students within governing bodies as well as securing the participation of students in task forces, committees and discussion forums outside the governance structures. The importance of increasing the commitment of the students to solve problems and push for reforms is mentioned as well as their participation in the Bologna Process. Other suggestions from the academic representatives are to try to increase the number of students as members of parliament and to introduce student questionnaires in order to evaluate the education and the lecturers.

Other comments to the questionnaire

Students, ministry representatives and academics underline the differences in legislation and practice between institutions or regions concerning student participation. This is primarily highlighted by countries with binary systems – different systems for universities and non-university institutions – or with both public and private higher education institutions within the national system. The particularities of the different systems provoke problems for some countries in answering the questionnaire and in the interpretation of the results of the survey. In some cases legislation has recently changed which also affects the answers to our questions.

Student and ministry representatives from several countries have mentioned difficulties in co-ordinating student participation and influence at national level. In two of the countries this is said to be because of federal systems and two other countries describe problems in keeping a national student union with a political mandate active and together. One of the ministry representatives considers the lack of a student counterpart at national level to be a problem. In other cases there are well-functioning national student organisations, but no legislation concerning student participation at national level.

One student representative states that the new higher education act in the country concerned actually reduces student influence at the institutional level generally, on institutional governance and relating to budget matters.

Both students and academic representatives mention that the students are not always as active in governance-related issues as would be desirable. Any actual student influence is also to a large extent as a result of the leadership of the institutions at the different governance levels.

One student representative raises the question of political pressures and influence on the student organisations at different levels. Student unions strongly dominated by political considerations at the institutional level are not considered to be of benefit for the development and protection of student rights.

Table: Countries and groups responding to the questionnaire[*]

	Students	Ministries	Academics
Albania			
Andorra	---	X	
Armenia	X		
Austria	X		X
Azerbaijan	---		
Belarus			X
Belgium, *Flemish Community*	X	X	
Belgium, *French Community*	X	X	X
Bosnia/Herzegovina			
Bulgaria	X		X
Croatia	XX	X	X
Cyprus	X	X	
Czech Republic			X
Denmark	X		X
Estonia	X	X	
Finland	XX	X	X
France			
Georgia			X
Germany	X	X	X
Greece		X	
Holy See			
Hungary	X	X	X
Iceland	X		X
Ireland			
Italy		X	X
Latvia	X	X	X
Liechtenstein		X	
Lithuania	X	X	X
Luxembourg			
Malta	X		X
Moldova	X		X
Netherlands	X		
Norway	XX	X	X
Poland			
Portugal	X		X
Romania	X		
Russian Federation	---		
San Marino	---		
Slovak Republic			

---

[*] Thirty-six countries represented.
Two answers from the same country in three student cases. Twenty-five countries with more than one group answering.

74

Slovenia	X	X	
Spain	X	X	X
Sweden	X	X	X
Switzerland	X	X	X
"The former Yugoslav Republic of Macedonia"	X		
Turkey	---		X
Ukraine			
United Kingdom			
Serbia and Montenegro – Serbia	X	X	
Serbia and Montenegro – Montenegro	X	X	X
TOTAL 73/76	**28/31**	**21**	**24**

Questionnaire

Part 1 Information on the respondent

Country: _____

Function:

- Student representative

- Ministry representative

- Academic representative

Part 2 Formal provisions for student participation in higher education governance based on national legislation

2.1   Does your country have legal or constitutional mechanisms to ensure student representation in higher education governance at the national level?

Yes   No

If yes, please
explain:_____

2.2   Does your country have legal mechanisms to ensure student representation and participation in the governance of higher education institutions?

Yes   No

If no, please proceed to Question 2.6.

2.3   If yes, at what levels of governance is student representation regulated by law or other means?
Please mark all relevant categories

Institutional level
Faculty level
Department/institute level
_____ (other)

2.4 Is there a minimum legal or constitutional requirement for student representation, for example as a *percentage* or a certain *number* of seats that have to be reserved for students within the board of the institution?

Yes   No
If yes, what percentage or number?

Percentage: 1-10   11-20   21-30   31-40   41-50   above 50
Number: _____
Other requirements: _____

2.5 Do the students have the right to vote in the governance bodies concerned?

Yes   No

If yes, does the right to vote cover all issues treated by the bodies concerned?

Yes   No   not at the level of/within the areas
of_____

2.6 Are the higher education institutions required by law/constitution/agreement to have a policy on student participation?

Yes   No   No, but most of them have

2.7 To your knowledge, are there policies within higher education institutions that ensure a *stronger* student participation in the governance than those required by law?

Yes   No

(Please feel free to describe any such examples on a separate page)

2.8 Are political student organisations at the higher education institutions legal?

Yes   No

2.9   How do you become a student representative?

        Directly elected   Indirectly elected   Appointed

        If appointed, by whom? _____

2.10   Are there laws or regulations concerning how student
        representatives should be elected?

        Yes   No

        If yes, what issues do the regulations concern?

        Minimum percentage of student electorate participating in the
        election
        Elections through secret ballot
        Other _____

2.11   Are student evaluations of courses and programmes required by law
        or other regulations?

        Yes   No

**Part 3 Other provisions for student participation in higher education
          governance**

3.1   Are there regular contacts between the government or the ministry
        responsible for higher education and student representatives, for
        example within a national forum on the Bologna Process?

        Yes   No

        If yes, are these contacts restricted to certain areas?

        Yes   which areas? _____   No

3.2   Is there student participation or representation in relation to the
        national rectors' conference or other equivalent bodies?

        Yes   No

3.3   Do student representatives or student bodies have regular informal or formal contact with the national parliamentary assembly?

Yes   No

3.4   Are there any other formal or informal procedures to ensure student influence on higher education governance at national level?

Yes   No

If yes, how? _____

_____

3.5   Is there a division of powers between student organisations at national level and at the institutional level concerning higher education governance?

Yes   No

If yes, in what way?

_____

_____

3.6   Is there regular communication between national and institutional student organisations on governance issues?

Yes   No

If yes, please describe:

_____

_____

Part 4   Actual practice of student participation

4.1   If there are legal provisions for student participation is it – in general – possible to find enough candidates to occupy all elective positions reserved for students?

Yes   No

If yes,why?_____

_____

4.2   Is there any level where there are particular problems finding
        candidates to occupy the seats reserved for students?
        Please mark all relevant categories

        National level
        Institutional level
        Faculty level
        Department/institute level
        _____ (other)

        No

4.3   How are candidates for student representatives in your country
        normally presented in the elections at the different levels?

        Level   *Institution*   *Faculty*   *Dep/Inst*

        Through non-political
        student organisations
        Through political student
        organisations
        Individual

4.4   Is a minimum number of signatures from the student electorate
        required?

        Yes, national level
        Yes, institutional level
        Yes, faculty level
        Yes, department/institute level
        Yes, _____ (other)

        No

4.5   What is, in general, the age of the student representatives?
        Indicate a maximum of two alternatives

        under 20   20-23   24-27   28-31   over 32

4.6   What is normally the percentage of students participating in the
        election of student representatives to university bodies or student
        organisations?

        0-15   16-30   31-45   46-60   61-75   more than 76

4.7   Are protocols and decisions from university governance meetings at different levels made public?

Yes   No

If no, please proceed to Question 4.9.

4.8   If yes, does the university administration take steps to disseminate information about such documents and decisions?

Yes   No

4.9   Do student organisations take steps to disseminate information about such documents and decisions?

Yes   No

4.10   In your opinion, how strong is the level of student influence on higher education?

Please, estimate the level of influence by indicating the appropriate number (1=Very weak, 5=Very strong)

At national level	1	2	3	4	5
At institutional level generally	1	2	3	4	5
On institutional governance	1	2	3	4	5
On budget matters	1	2	3	4	5
On pedagogical issues	1	2	3	4	5
On educational content issues	1	2	3	4	5
On criteria for the employment of teaching staff	1	2	3	4	5
On criteria for the admission of students	1	2	3	4	5
On social and environmental issues at the institution	1	2	3	4	5

4.11   At which level of governance do you consider students to have the strongest influence?

Please rank the levels so that Number 1 should indicate that this is the level where you consider students to have the strongest influence, 2 should indicate the level where they have the second strongest influence etc.

National level   ___
Institutional level   ___
Faculty level   ___
Department/institute level   ___
_____ (other)   ___

4.12   In your opinion, should the student influence in higher education
       governance increase?

       Yes   No

       If yes, why?
       _____
       _____
       How?_____
       _
       _____

       If no, why not?
       _____
       _____

Other comments you may wish to add:_____
_____

Thank you for your kind co-operation!

The university as site of citizenship

Frank Plantan

Introduction

The initiative: background and context

The concept of sites of citizenship originates with the Council of Europe project on Education for Democratic Citizenship (EDC). The project, the operational phase of which ended in 2000, was launched in 1996 and was adapted in the light of the Council of Europe Second Summit of Heads of State and Government in 1997. It was expected that the sites' network of the EDC project would continue after the formal completion of the project. This network would also have a higher education input.

The concept of Education for Democratic Citizenship was taken a considerable step further through the Budapest Declaration for a Greater Europe Without Dividing Lines, adopted on the occasion of the fiftieth anniversary of the Council of Europe in May 1999, and in particular through the Declaration and Programme on Education for Democratic Citizenship, based on the Rights and Responsibilities of Citizens.

The declaration and programme adopted in Budapest underline, among other things, the fundamental role of education in promoting the active participation of all individuals in democratic life at all levels, the importance of learning about democracy in school and university life, including participation in the decision-making process and the associated structures of students and teachers.

As a follow-up to one of its preliminary contributions to the definition of the concept of citizenship, the Council of Europe's Higher Education and Research Committee (CC-HER)[62] adopted, at its 6th plenary session from 16 to 18 March 1999, an outline project called University as Site of Citizenship and instructed its bureau and its secretariat to develop the project further.

At the same time academic circles in the United States of America became involved in the development of projects concerning citizenship within higher education institutions. The CC-HER bureau established close co-operative links with those circles. In addition to the importance of such co-operation, it is worth underlining the fact that the US now has general Observer status with the Council of Europe, including Observer status with the CD-ESR.

The concern of the US academic community for the matter of citizenship within higher education institutions has been expressed through the

---

[62] The CC-HER has since become the Steering Committee for Higher Education and Research (CD-ESR).

Wingspread Declaration on Renewing the Civic Mission of the American Research University (December 1998) and the President's Fourth of July Declaration on the Civic Responsibility of Higher Education (President's Leadership Colloquium convened by Campus Compact and the American Council on Education at the Aspen Institute from 29 June to 1 July 1999).

As a result, two parallel projects – which could be seen as a single project – were launched in Europe and in the United States under the auspices of the Higher Education and Research Committee of the Council of Europe and a consortium of European and US researchers and institutional representatives.

Aims of the project

The project was established to:

- consider the actual activities of institutions of higher education in Europe and the US that support democratic values and practices;
- assess their capabilities and dispositions to promote democratic political developments;
- make recommendations and disseminate resources in order to improve the contribution of higher education to democracy on campus, and to the local community, and society in general.

Methodology

Establishing the project

Following the recommendations of the CC-HER and its bureau, a Working Group was set up, responsible for outlining and carrying out the project.

The Working Group decided to launch a pilot project with the following objectives:

- to map current activities and problems in education for democratic citizenship within higher education institutions;
- to collect information from the target groups (students, faculty members, administrative staff) through pre-tested questionnaires and guidelines;
- to produce case study reports detailing the variety of problems and successes.

Fifteen European universities were selected among new and old democracies and fifteen collaborating researchers (making up a Contact Group) were appointed who were responsible for conducting the case studies. They reported their findings through monographs to the general rapporteur who was responsible for producing the final report.

The organisation of the case studies was aided by the use of questionnaires and guidelines drawn up by the Working Group. An interesting quantity of information was collected during this exercise that took place in thirteen of the fifteen European institutions selected at the beginning of the project and fourteen US institutions.

Time scales

The pilot project covered the period from March 1999 to March 2001 and was carried out in the following stages:

- At its plenary session from 16 to 18 March 1999, the Higher Education and Research Committee (CC-HER) adopted the outline project and mandated its bureau and the secretariat to develop it further.

- In May 1999, the CC-HER received additional funding for follow-up action to the Second Summit, making the financing of the project possible; in the US the National Science Foundation decided to finance the American part of the project.

- In September 1999, the CC-HER bureau decided to appoint a Working Party for the project.

- On behalf of the Working Group, the chair of the CC-HER established contacts with US academic circles.

- The Working Group met on 17 September 1999 to consider in detail the scope of the project and the modalities for financing it.

- The Working Group held a joint meeting on 22 October 1999 with collaborating researchers from six European universities in order to launch the case studies; US representatives attended the meeting.

- The Working Group held a joint meeting on 11 February 2000 with collaborating researchers from nine European universities; US representatives attended the meeting.

- Drafting of student/faculty questionnaires and guidelines by the Working Group from October 1999 to March 2000.

- At its 7th plenary session from 28 to 30 March 2000, the Higher Education and Research Committee (CC-HER) noted the progress report on the project and approved its further plans. It further noted that it would decide on a possible large-scale follow-up project at its 2001 plenary session, on the basis of the outcomes of the pilot project.

- The case studies were launched in fifteen European universities as well as in fifteen US universities in March 2000. They were completed by the end of July 2000.

- The Working Group and the Contact Group held a joint meeting on 11 and 12 December 2000 to consider the final results of the European and American case studies; US representatives attended the meeting.

- Drafting of the preliminary version of the general report of the pilot project from January to March 2001.

The final version of the general report was submitted to the plenary session of the CD-ESR in October 2001, which asked the Working Group to discuss it in greater detail and to propose follow-up activities.

Organisation and approach to the research

The remit of this project was to determine the actual activities and capacities of universities in education for democracy. The project maps the variety of what was being done in universities to promote citizenship, and hence, democracy; and therefore, to assess the civic responsibility of institutions of higher education in contributing to these outcomes.

The collection of information about universities and their localities in relation to the aims of this project noted above was aided by the use of questionnaires and guidelines. The collaborating researcher responsibilities were quite broad and included the gathering of official documents, conducting interviews, soliciting official statements and policies from relevant officials, and collecting survey data.

At the conclusion of these efforts each researcher was asked to write a narrative of about fifteen pages highlighting the main features of democracy at the university and its locality. The focus of this monograph was on what is *not* present in the institution or revealed in the accumulated documentary evidence or survey data.

The format and substance of this narrative was up to the researcher, keeping in mind that this pilot project was designed to map the variety of democratic experiences, or their opposite, within universities and the place where they are located.

The information necessary to meet the demands of these guidelines was documentary, in the form of records, publications, or official policy statements, and in the minds of the selected informants (their experience and knowledge). The guidelines were in three parts as follows:

- the first involved interviews with individuals from targeted groups in the university and community. The interviews were designed as a source of information for the third part (summary);
- the second involved a group of interviews with twenty students and twenty academic staff;
- the third was a summary report, an evaluative narrative of what the university was doing in education on democracy not only within the university but also within its locality.

The questionnaires focused on three main discussion topics:

- student participation in university governance;
- university teaching;
- relations with community environment.

Highlights of the findings

Any attempt to summarise the disparate findings of so many institutions, chosen to capture the diversity in higher education in Europe, poses special challenges. Because of the vast differences in size, demographic composition, financial basis and legal incorporation, each site report confirmed the unique aspects of civic engagement on each campus. These reports present an amalgam of findings, the differences and similarities of which are outlined in the report that follows. A few generalisations can be made however, with the caveat that the applicability and relevance of each point will vary by institution. A discussion of more institution-specific findings follows.

Salient points/summary

- While national political and ethnic context is important to the development of new approaches to the teaching of citizenship and democracy, these contexts can also be barriers to change where cultural and historical relativism postulate that each national situation is unique.

- Universities as cultural institutions are embedded in society and, therefore, reforms intended to promote democratic values or greater civic engagement can conflict with the traditional role of universities as providers of "useful" education.

- In addition to historical and cultural traditions, the legal and institutional framework universities operate in, and their effect on the larger issues embraced by this study (participation, civic responsibility, civic engagement, democratic education), are critical to understanding the degree of freedom an institution has in promoting these values.

- The legal and statutory framework of universities determines the parameters that universities must work within when attempting reforms or implementing new policies or means to promote a greater degree of civic engagement. Academic and administrative leadership of universities can choose not only the mechanisms for change, but also determine the amount of latitude they can take in effecting new initiatives based on their interpretation and enforcement of these statutes.

- Formal and statutory provisions for shared governance, transparency of decision making and protection of faculty and student rights are often at odds with reality and actual practices.

- Traditional social and professional relationships between administration, faculty and students, rooted in cultural expectations create inertia against change even when statutory provisions are made for greater participation and inclusion.

- Sustainability of initiatives for change and promotion of democracy and civic responsibility are affected by the availability of resources, the larger national economic conditions, and the onset of intellectual fatigue for political action.

- Formal institutional structures and arrangements are a *necessary*, but *not sufficient* condition for:

    – greater democratic participation in both university politics and governance and in the community and society by students;

    – the promotion of aims and objectives of instilling notions of civic responsibility in students;

    – understanding the nature and extent of a university's interaction with its surrounding community;

    – curricular change and altering the management functions within the university.

- Despite provision for formal organisational roles and rights for both faculty and students at most institutions in the study, participation in governance processes is not what might be hoped for and expected. Many researchers noted the existence of misunderstanding or lack of knowledge among respondents of organisational and administrative processes within universities that further limited possibilities for greater participation.

- Informal personal networks and peer learning play a major role in what students know about their rights. These interactions also shape their expectations regarding their rights, their understandings about what possibilities exist for them to participate in university governance or decision making, and in the ways in which they learn and internalise notions of civic responsibility and democracy.

- Most sites reported that university administrators and many faculty considered many aspects of citizenship and democracy to be entirely a personal matter; such as decisions to vote, to volunteer in the community, to participate in campus organisations, or to engage in political debate and, therefore, not within their ken nor responsibilities as teachers and scholars.

- As a corollary to the previous point, most university administrators and faculty considered institutional responses to promoting democratic values and civic engagement as an infringement upon or a dilution of the university's primary educational mission, such as the training of specialists and technicians and other professionals.

- Any attempts to better understand the problems of democratic and civic education must come to grips with the problem of fragmentation. Students and faculty have "separate lives" outside the university and often segregate their social roles and actions between life within and without the university.

- Segregation of roles and responsibilities also affects the role of the university vis-à-vis the community and/or the nation. How the university conceives its role vis-à-vis society and the local community affects its response to social and political trends. It also determines how these issues and policies are engaged by the university.

- There is a problem of a status quo based on complacency, comfort, indifference and inefficacy. In stable situations where students are content with their life, they believe as one respondent reported, "what's the point of using democracy through the university?"[63]

- Student participation in university governance and in asserting or understanding their rights as students are characterised by a *pervasive passivity* bordering on indifference. This was true across almost every case in the study.

---

[63] There is a certain tautology expressed here between this finding and the inferred hypotheses and motivations for this study. Are political stability (or certainty) and general comfort and wellbeing causally related to inefficacy and indifference, or are they intervening variables between socialisation and educational processes that political socialisation research postulates shapes the predispositions and behaviour of students in terms of their political participation and sense of civil responsibility?

Summary of site reports

Characteristics of campuses

The universities selected for this pilot study, while not randomly selected, do represent a geographical diversity that has characterised the emergence and growth of European universities since the founding of the universities in Bologna and Paris. The universities in this study vary from prominent, old, established institutions to newly created institutions growing along with the municipalities where they are sited. Some are located in wealthy nations sheltered by the political stability of the European Union, and others are in what are commonly referred to as "transitional" countries, struggling with radical and rapid social, political and economic change. Still others pursue their educational mission in the context of civil strife, reconstruction from war, and the depravations that accompany conflict. Yet all share profound similarities, such as a universal educational mission in the production of knowledge, human capital and technical expertise in service to the nation.

They also share similar difficulties. These difficulties differ only in scale between institutions. Universities face new and special difficulties in finance and budgeting; in their relationship to their surrounding community; in developing and maintaining the requisite infrastructure to meet their educational mission; and in reforming and adapting new institutional structures, processes, and programmes in response to the changes in borders, governments, and the political economy of Europe of the last decade.

A brief survey of the universities studied is illustrative of their differences and provides a backdrop for analysis and conclusions. Uniqueness does not mean they do not share experiences, or that common approaches in administrative policies, practices and reforms to promote democratic values and an enhanced sense of civil responsibility cannot be achieved. Similarities in mission, faculty-student relationships, administrative organisation, and relationships to government overview and funding agencies provide much common ground for understanding and benefiting from comparative research. The location of the university's site and the distribution of its buildings is an important characteristic for understanding its relationship with the community. Together with the composition and size of the student body, and residential options available, it shapes both the internal and external environment of the university.

Many university sites, particularly urban ones, are dispersed throughout the surrounding community, and therefore, defy traditional notions of the "campus." The University of Tuzla, in Bosnia and Herzegovina is spread over the entire town in which it is located. It is one of the main universities in the national system. About a third of its students are part-time or correspondence students. All of its students are local in origin with few foreign students to speak of. The government plays a major role in funding and regulating the affairs of the school. The university was reconstituted under a new higher education law in 1999.

Similarly, the University of Cergy-Pontoise, in France, has its buildings spread throughout the community. It is a very young campus of ten years. It is suburban, part of the Paris metropolitan area. What is distinctive is that the town has over thirty ethnic and foreign groups residing in it. Eighty percent of its students are from the local region. It has a small but growing number of foreign students. Its links with the local government are very strong, almost symbiotic. The closeness of this relationship and the dominance of the university in local affairs and culture make it a quintessential university town.

The University of Tirana, in Albania, is located in the capital city, benefiting from the advantages of its location by enriching the life and opportunities of its students, faculty and staff. It is the national university and enjoys the privileges of being "the largest, the most consolidated, most complete and best quality university in Albania."[64]

The University of Milano-Bicocca, in Italy, is new, only three years old. It has been part of the "hyperactive" growth and building in the old industrial district of this city of 8 million people. It literally grew overnight and has a large population of 27 000 students. Though thought of as a "campus" university because of the clustering of its buildings, it has no residential facilities. Students are commuters and live in the city.

The University of Vytauti Magni, in Lithuania, has ancient roots with its original incorporation traced back 423 years. It has been reorganised and reconstituted several times as a result of historical changes in the geopolitical situation of Lithuania. Most recently, it has been reconstituted under new statutes as part of the "national revival" campaign following the country's independence.

The University of Samara, in the Russian Federation, is a maturing institution founded in 1969 in a large industrial city. Today, the city confronts the duality of deteriorating economy and infrastructure, though it has a "high market potential" (that is, a net donor to central government) because of oil enterprises and a strong agricultural base. Samara has a 2:1 female/male student ratio and is very homogeneous (all Russian), with students who are inhabitants of the region.

The University of Thessaly, in Greece, is also relatively new, taking its first students in 1989. It is characterised by a historically powerful rector who is now elected by and accountable to the university senate. Most of the university's departments are located in the town of Volos, with others spread through other locations. Thessaly is an industrial region in Greece with a changing economic base. Many regard the establishment of the university as an imposition and relations with the community have been marked by strife and suspicion of the university and in the interactions between residents and students.

---

[64] DGIV/EDU/HE (2000), University of Tirana, Albania, p. 7. The quote refers to the description given in the report and should not be considered as a quality assessment by the Council of Europe.

The University of Bergen, in Norway, was established following the Second World War. It is in the second largest city in Norway (but small relative to others on the continent, with a population of 250 000). Changing national demographics and the standardisation of the curriculum in Norwegian higher education has led to a large increase in the student population in recent years.

The University of Skopje, in "the former Yugoslav Republic of Macedonia", is a large, urban, comprehensive research university. It, too, was reorganised following independence and creation of a new constitution. It is now more autonomous and increasingly places emphasis on merit for access and participation in the management of the institution.

The University of Ankara, in Turkey, is a large, urban, secular university located in the old capital city. As the flagship university of Turkey it works in close conjunction and partnership with the government and non-governmental organisations (NGOs) to support local and national policies through teaching and research and joint outreach programmes with the community.

The Tavrichesky National University of Ukraine is also a large institution and the main university of the Crimea. Because of its mission of service to the Crimea and its population, its facilities are dispersed over fourteen towns. It has a large number of correspondence-course students.

Queen's University, Belfast, in the United Kingdom (Northern Ireland), was founded as one of the three main universities of Ireland. Today it is a comprehensive research university, situated in the vibrant and popular south side of Belfast near the centre of the city. It is also surrounded by the major cultural institutions of Belfast, a city that witnessed a quarter of a century of violent ethno-religious political conflict.

This is a large and diverse group of institutions, culturally and historically bound in their national context. How can we generalise or find commonalities among such diversity? Certainly there is no way to describe the "average" of these institutions. If we cannot identify many common experiences, then what can be learned from the other's experience? We look not only for common experiences, but common difficulties, which is perhaps the more important task of a pilot study such as this. Developing inventories of democratic policies and practices and of what forms of civic engagement universities are currently pursuing provides the baseline for new initiatives. These inventories also provide the basis for comparing the diverse group of universities participating in the study. Can the Turkish example of educational reform in the context of its modernisation drive help university officials and policy makers better understand the challenges for Bosnia, Albania, Lithuania etc.? Can the size, stage of development, financial situation, or the cultural and historical constraints of an institution inform other universities of ways to address similar issues in their local context?

The practical necessity to find answers to these rhetorical questions rests in the development of shared concepts of citizenship and civic responsibility; democracy and democratic values that facilitate a stronger European identity and prosperity while protecting and maintaining the rich intellectual and cultural traditions of each nation. Professor Alain Renault encapsulated this ambition when he noted that:

> "[I]f it were deemed a good idea to enrich the intellectual and cultural education systems specific to each country by adding a common element through which, as part of the learning process, a number of values and principles could be shared, universities would seem to be the most apt institution to fulfil this function."[65]

This study continues the exploration begun by others of how democratic citizenship can be made possible in an increasing multicultural context and differing national needs.

The political environment of universities

The political context and environment of a country strongly relates to the delivery of higher education, and to the organisation and activities of universities as sites of citizenship. In addition, the legal context defines the parameters of what universities can and cannot do. For example, in what might appear to be ironic to more mature democracies, many newly independent and transitional countries place legal prohibitions on political activities within the university. This is especially the case in contexts shaped by conflict where maintenance of the peace and civil society takes precedence over the promotion of political debate. Many of the institutions studied also exhibited a primacy of culture and history over principles of political participation, political organisation, and even the principle of pluralism.

In several institutions the majority of faculties considered the support of national goals as a primary mission of the university. This seemed even more apparent in the transitional countries and those having suffered war or violent civil unrest (Queen's University, Belfast is an exception in this regard). Human rights concerns in some countries also took primacy over the day-to-day processes and interactions of democratic life or the promotion of civic responsibility.

A university's ability to sustain initiatives for greater participation in the political life of the community and the decision-making and governance of the university is shaped by larger historical political and economic factors. For example, following the demise of the dictatorship in Greece in 1974, student activism reached its peak. Many changes in the organisation of universities resulted and in the development of student rights. At the University of Thessaly today, students are regarded as being apathetic and

---

[65] Alain Renaut, "The role of universities in developing a democratic European culture," in *Concepts of Democratic Citizenship*, Strasbourg: Council of Europe Publishing, 2000, p. 99.

not fully availing themselves of the rights won by earlier generations of students. More recently, at the University of Vytauti Magni in Lithuania, during the "national revival" period, there was very high political activity and civic engagement in an effort to resurrect national traditions and increase student awareness. This has been followed by an extended period of less activity as students become more preoccupied with their immediate living needs and future vocations. The site researcher reported on the need to re-focus the university mission as the hardships of transition begin to reduce aspirations. Societal factors (ruling parties, corruption, unemployment, crime, etc.) increasingly impinge on the motivations and calculations of students and have cooled enthusiasm for change. Because of these factors young people have an incentive to emigrate, making it all the more critical for those that stay to receive a high quality education that is relevant to their needs. The university, in consequence, despite its new openness and promotion of democratic practices, must renew its concentration on its traditional and primary mission of training and education to meet the vocational needs of students and the human capital needs of society.

This phenomenon is being witnessed at several of the university sites. It could be a major obstacle to teaching democracy and citizenship, because of the overwhelming need to meet the vocational interests and demands of students, whose most salient concern appears to be to ensure employment and relevant work following graduation. External pressures are also put on universities to intensify their focus on meeting national needs and in the demand for specialists and technicians. At the University of Samara, for example, the rector was chosen not only to help lead the university, but to help co-ordinate the use of university resources and personnel with city officials to facilitate the challenges of transition to a market-based economy. As a consequence, the university has become more deeply connected throughout the locale and region. Similarly, Tavrichesky National University in Ukraine was reorganised in 1999 under a new higher education law that implies an "internal logic" intending to facilitate the connection of the university to the problems of transition to a market economy.

In contrast, a more sustained, long-term effort occurred at the University of Ankara suggesting that democracy and civic education do not have to be sacrificed to larger social and political pressures. According to the site researcher, Ankara has confronted the changes in organisational structure and academic programmes to meet the demands for human rights and democratisation through the nation's process of modernisation. The driving force in this effort has been a reorganisation of the education system in conjunction with the government's efforts to expand its relationship with the European Union by putting tolerance, freedom and individual rights at the centre of education. The University of Ankara is continuing to develop programmes and initiatives, often in conjunction with international organisations and NGOs, to meet international standards by facilitating the alignment of domestic laws and institutions with these standards.

The Ankara example is instructive in the connections it makes between the democratic and civil society agenda of universities with larger societal apolitical and economic purposes. This is an important residual macro-social effect of teaching and research targeted at students and individuals in the university and surrounding community. Arguments that the pursuit of the twin agendas of democracy education and civic engagement is fundamental to larger social, political and economic transformations and gains are usually couched in theoretical terms. This case, and others in the study such as the experiences of Queen's University, Belfast, suggest concrete connections between a university's democratic education mission and societal-level benefits.

Prohibition of political parties and their activities

Another structural characteristic of universities is the legal and administrative prescriptions regarding organised political activity within the university. Many institutions in this study, particularly those in transitional societies or who have recently experienced violent conflict, are attempting to respond to new statutory and constitutional arrangements. They are struggling with redefining roles and responsibilities while simultaneously dealing with basic issues of meeting their educational mission within tight fiscal and budgetary constraints.

At the universities of Tirana and Tuzla, university-affiliated people may belong to political parties and organisations as long as their party work is outside the person's university functions; that is, in their normal capacity as a citizen. At these institutions, any student participation in politics is a matter of personal choice and is not encouraged or discouraged by the university ("life of students outside their normal activities is not a matter of interest to the University").[66] More specifically, at the University of Tirana political parties are restricted. Since the revolution, universities are considered to be de-politicised by statutory requirement. This is considered a "victory for democracy" because in the past the university was compelled to indoctrinate youth in communist ideology as part of its educational mission. Likewise, at the University of Vytauti Magni, no political parties are allowed. Students and faculty who engage in political party activities do so outside the university in their capacity as private citizens. At the University of Samara, Russian national constitutional law prohibits activities of political organisations on campus. In consequence, "...political life in the university is minimal".[67]

Contrasting these situations with countries with no ban risks simplification of the social, cultural and historical differences of the universities: the age of the institution, the nation's experience with democracy, and general social stability. But the expectation that there would be greater political activity at institutions where there is no ban does not appear to be true in most cases. Even at institutions where political organisations are not prohibited, political activity among students is not much greater. In fact, student political activity could be characterised as somnambulant. At the University of Thessaly, few students are involved in political parties. There is little political party activity on campus because, according to the site researcher, students are simply

---

[66] DGIV/EDU/HE (2000), University of Tirana, Albania report, p. 14.
[67] Ibid., University of Samara, Russia report, p. 101.

apolitical in their general orientation and life. Across the Adriatic, in the Italian context, political parties are not restricted at Milano-Biccoca. Also, there is not much public debate on campus, even though there is some departmental activity that would encourage discussion of political issues. At Biccoca, both student activists and non-activists reported that groups that promote democratic participation do not have a large following among the student body. Most declare themselves to be independent of political parties while faculty describe their political actions within the university as being independent of political party affiliation. This latter point hardly seems unusual and contrasts the distinction between party identification and party membership. Many individuals would describe themselves as having a party identification (Social Democrat, Christian Democrat, or Green) but their political actions or advocacy may not be the result of party affiliation or party-directed activity.

At Tavrichesky National University its educational mission includes "defending culture and education from political experiments".[68] While there are no restrictions on political activity, none occurs. The atmosphere is stultified by constraints imposed by government and administration and reinforced by the vocational orientation of apolitical students. The University of Skopje does not have political organisations on campus, though it is not clear if they are banned. Students get involved in political organisations outside the campus through political party youth organisations. Also, students are very active in NGOs for the promotion of democracy in the entire society.[69]

The increasing role played by NGOs at universities is becoming recognised by universities as a means of pursuing or complementing their objectives. NGOs play a facilitating role in several institutions. At Ankara, NGOs work in partnership with the university for the promotion of human rights and democracy and work closely with universities to advance their agenda. At Tavrichesky National, NGOs can even be established in the university with material university support as long as their activities are in keeping with the university mission. Because the University of Tirana is located in the capital it is able to take advantage of all other activities, seminars, conferences etc., available in the city and because of the presence of these resources the university is making more vigorous efforts to co-ordinate its efforts with other agencies and NGOs located in the city.

Administrative practices and university leadership

The range of options and parameters for change in a university is largely determined by the roles and responsibilities of the authorities that govern and manage universities including a university's central administration, local government officials, and the ministry of education. Statutory and other legal provisions further delineate and constrain options and action. These factors together can also be a source of institutional inertia by protecting an

---

[68] Ibid., Tavrichesky National University, Ukraine report, p. 149.
[69] Ibid., University of Skopje, "the former Yugoslav Republic of Macedonia" report, p. 128.

institution's cultural traditions, or by establishing excessive or arbitrary bureaucratic impediments to change.

Generally, most administrators were supportive and co-operative with the project by providing catalogues, mission statements, programme brochures and other materials to the Contact Group. In learning of the purpose of the project, some university administrators became very interested in how this pilot study might advance other related civic education projects they had started on their campuses. For example, some already have a civic education agenda and more have an interest in human rights and democracy education to help meet criteria for European Union admission. Also, many administrators reported interest in implementation problems and how to deal with legal changes and conflicts of laws.[70]

In transitional countries changes in administrative organisation and practices were generally acknowledged as improvements since independence, though as noted below, these changes have not completely altered many bureaucratic practices or authoritative styles of leadership. More importantly, many perceive that the social changes in society made and continue to make a difference in terms of restructuring of university management, the orientation of the university to its surrounding community, and the redefinition of its mission in service to society. However, many of these efforts at working with the community or serving the nation were based on the actions of faculty and administrators working as individuals, and less in terms of an organised institutional response to societal needs.

This can be seen, for example, in the University of Tirana report, which noted that the university still "lacks a concept of management", and where certain officials still exercise arbitrariness, particularly in employment practices. A few individuals continue to dominate the decision-making process. There is little public notice of decisions and less discussion and debate within the university community, hence, there is little accountability (in terms of challenging decisions or explaining the basis of decisions). Many institutions are still characterised by a rigid hierarchical structure, with a rector appointed by the ministry of education and having significant authority to make decisions in the absence of shared governance traditions. The general perception among faculty and students throughout all the cases in this study was that power is concentrated at the top and most decisions in the university are made by a few individuals.

Students are rarely, if ever, consulted. The University of Bergen, for example, is marked by the administration's failure to consult students. There are no public hearings on university decisions. Similar perceptions exist at the University of Thessaly where excessively bureaucratic approaches to student quality-of-life issues has created tension and resentment. There needs to be a stronger awareness that administrative style is as important as administrative structures as it affects students' attitudes toward good citizenship because of poor modelling of behaviour. This remains true at

---

[70] This was reported during the Contact Group meeting in December 2000, but not explicitly noted in reports.

most institutions studied. Student participation in governance of universities is generally weak. Even where formal rights exist for inclusion of students in governing bodies, most students at nearly all institutions surveyed expressed disenchantment with the university's practices and lack of communication. Most also do not feel they are consulted on matters of university governance. In many ways this comes as no surprise and may be endemic to the structure of university decision making because of the relatively short academic lifespan of students. Students are transient and move through their academic programmes and the institution with relative speed, whereas faculty and administrators endure at an institution through multiple academic generations. Faculty and administrators represent the institutional memory of a university, which is particularly important in the decision-making process where many issues are recurring and institutional history is important in establishing context. This may help to explain the apparent lack of input by students in university governance (further discussed below).

There is also a certain irony in contrasting participation opportunities for students with university administrator's beliefs. Students claim they take little part in nor have much opportunity to participate in university decision making while administrators tended to point to the existence of opportunities – usually highlighting formal legal arrangements – and other efforts to be more inclusive. In most universities the perception remains, however, of widespread student feelings of inefficacy (Samara, Vytauti Magni, and Queen's seem to be exceptions). The example of Queen's University, Belfast, shows that leadership matters. Both the chancellor and vice-chancellor there have distinguished records of collegial leadership and in conflict resolution. This not only sets the tone for proper democratic demand and problem solving, such leadership typically directs the university mission towards meeting the objectives of civic education and democracy in its education programmes.

Changes in the external environment, such as changes in funding sources or the amount of funding allocated to the university, impacts the administrative decision making of universities. As pressures increase for more efficient management of universities, concerns are growing over how a more corporate model of the university might affect the promotion of democracy and civic education.

Formal provisions versus actual practice

One of the most consistent findings throughout the site reports was the disjunction between formal, constitutional and statutory provisions for participation and input by students and faculty into university decisions and governance, and the actual practices of universities. Perceptions among faculty and students were even more at odds with reality and are perhaps more important because they represent the institutional climate and mindsets that produce a heightened sense of disillusionment, and therefore, higher levels of political cynicism and personal inefficacy. These conclusions extend both to matters of university governance and decision making, and to student organisations and self-government. The few exceptions to this generalisation highlight the possibilities that exist for strengthening shared governance structures in universities in a way that facilitates the learning of democracy and acquiring norms of civic responsibility through practice and experience within the university itself.

A brief inventory of some details from the site reports illustrate these themes. In the most extreme instance of student distance from the governance process, in Ankara there are not even formal arrangements for student representation in university governance. There is indirect influence through the student union and its representatives. However, the students are poorly organised and not very representative of the wider student body. The university is not making any attempt to improve student governance bodies, or to expand their input into university governance.

At Tuzla, students have an equal vote in the Council of Academic Staff and can propose agenda items and vote. These privileges, however, appear to be only nominal either by virtue of the lack of voting strength or because students are marginalised or unable to exert any influence on decision making. Students themselves report a high degree of inefficacy or cynicism about this process. As many as 75% of respondents indicated that students are not consulted on issues of university governance. However, the site researcher reported that they do not need to be consulted because they are included in the decision-making process that is "pluralistic". It was unclear what this meant in the context of the university's governance processes.

At Thessaly, the presence of students is generally considered simply a formality to fulfil statutory requirements. However, while not effective centrally, students have more input and impact at departmental level, perhaps because of closer relationships with teaching staff. Students feel they are not consulted in governance issues and participation in governance if the university is weak. Such too was the case at Samara, which had formal arrangements for student participation but likewise found that students disagreed on their effectiveness.

At Biccoca, this is taken a step further with mandatory student representation (15% of total student body) on departmental committees. However, despite this presence, students do not count towards a quorum for substantive votes and decisions, and are excluded from deliberations on teaching and research appointments. Formal arrangements for student inclusion in university governance are clearly demarcated at various levels of administration at Biccoca. "Nearly all information to participate actively" in the university's democratic life is available on its Internet website. However, despite these arrangements and considerable information made available to them, Biccoca students do not consider the election of their representatives an important event (less than 12% turn out to vote in student elections). Student representatives are well known among the students though perceived to have little influence. According to the site researcher, the university is more adept at gathering information on student attitudes and opinions than in including them in the deliberative process. At Biccoca, the rector and university senate, the main deliberative organ with a role in funding allocations and human resources, makes most decisions. The senate includes student representation with incentives for students to vote because low voter turnout (less than 8%) results in a decrease in the number of student seats. Also, there is a pervasive sense that there is a lack of mechanisms available for expression of the student viewpoint (despite representation on many committees). A lack of efficacy is widespread among students – yet also, there is no sense of great dissatisfaction either.

Similar results were reported at Bergen. Students there are aware of formal structures and the mechanisms of representation, but are seriously sceptical about the efficacy of their participation and influence. This attitude was surprising at an institution with a highly politicised student body where the election of representatives to university governing bodies is organised around political groupings. These perceptions, however, were not shared by the faculty, who clearly disagreed that some groups are excluded from university life and governance. Here we see a significant gap between faculty and student attitudes. These differences between formal provisions for input and shared governance was described at Thessaly as a "democratic deficit", despite a statutory structure that provided for student representation.[71] The students do not take advantage of what is available to them, and the university does not consult with students. The researcher reported that students have full voting rights, yet a huge perception-reality gap exists between what statutes allow and what is practised. At some point student roles became only a kind of nominal representation. The current trend is that students see the university as becoming less open and transparent in its decision making. Where students do have input is usually on secondary issues. Formal administrative arrangements are nominally democratic, but practice reveals a different reality.

Some institutions have a greater degree of student influence on decision making. At Vytauti Magni the President of the Student Union is a "full and equal member of the rectorate".[72] However, even with this level of input and influence, half of the students and faculty reporting thought student participation is not effective. The experience at Cergy-Pontoise suggests that voting rights are not the only means of participating in decisions and governance. Consultative capacities can have as much influence on decisions, if the administration truly values and solicits student input. On the major decision-making body at Cergy-Pontoise, (*Conseil d'Administration* (CA)) students have only a consultative role. At lower levels as well, on the *Conseil des Etudes et de la Vie Universitaire* (CEVU), students have a consultative role. Yet, students are perceived to have strong representation. The CA-CEVU link is seen as vital to developing the democratic experience. New doctoral organisation at Cergy-Pontoise is expected to produce greater student involvement in direct decision making, with its own governing body. Administrators, however, reported that student involvement is only superficially democratic. There is dialogue, but no real demands. The site researcher suggests that this is perhaps attributable to lack of training, maturity or objective goals among students.

---

[71] DGIV/EDU/HE (2000), University of Thessaly, Greece report, p. 54.
[72] Ibid., University of Vytauti Magni, Lithuania report, p. 82.

This is a key issue and not unlike the situation in universities in the United States. The effectiveness of student input often depends on the attitude of the leadership. Simple consultation can have a greater impact on decision making than voting rights, depending on institutional and leadership orientation and beliefs and faculty interests and attitudes towards including students in the teaching and learning process and decisions surrounding them.

At Skopje students took a more active position. Student representatives from the student union are members of the university senate and are demanding an even greater degree of representation. Still, overall, most students view their participation in the management of the university as not effective and see the university's governance as poor. While extensive legal provisions are made, there has not been transference of legal provisions into reality. Such legal provisions therefore become an "alibi" for "real" democratisation in the university.[73] Student representation at Tirana included an allocation of 10% of the membership in university governance bodies ("real" representation of student's views claimed). This was seen as necessary because there are no student bodies for student self-governance.

At Tuzla, students were found to be generally dissatisfied with the governance of the university and their lack of input into university decision making. Moreover, it was reported that the administration is little concerned with the interests or demands of students. Several reports noted that students are mainly concerned with social and student life matters outside the university, which may explain in part their lack of attention to or concern for participation in the governance of the university. At Samara, students historically focused mainly on social matters. This was of course also attributable to the rigid, authoritarian governance structure of the university at the time, which left students little but to focus on social and student life issues. With legal and statutory changes it was expected that Samara would become more open, but now contradictions exist as although the administration espouses the desire to include students in university governance, there does not seem to be any substance to it. Faculty, too, do not perceive student involvement in governance as very high or effective. Traditional social and professional arrangements are difficult to change.

At Skopje, the climate is shaped by strong traditions that place the faculty at the centre of the university. The academic staff is considered "sacrosanct". There is a long tradition of faculty immunity and power over students. While the Skopje report was the only one to be this explicit about the organisational culture of the faculty in universities, one could infer that this tradition is pervasive throughout European higher education. This produces the classic "anticipated response" among students, resulting in self-censorship and self-regulation or silencing of student complaints.

Even with statutory and other organisational changes, many institutions still retained an authoritarian style of management and strict hierarchies. Ankara has a hierarchical system that reaches up to the ministry of education.

---

[73] Ibid., University of Skopje, Macedonia report, p. 126.

Transparency, though, is at least nominally guaranteed through formal processes and communication with departments at lower levels. It was not possible to judge the extent to which it is functionally transparent, especially since governance meetings are closed to the public. Likewise, Tavrichesky National also implemented a system of "self-governance" of the university because of changes in state law, but it has resulted in only nominal changes since most of the administrative and bureaucratic mechanisms for managing the university are unchanged since the Soviet era.

Government role in university administration

The government role in the management of universities remains very significant throughout Europe. In most places, government funding accounts for most of the current expense or regular budget. Even as some universities are being pressed by the government to identify and acquire new sources of funding and income, government funding formulas continue to constrain priority setting and, in turn, the degree to which faculty and students could have input into the allocation of resources on campus.

In some countries (for example Bosnia and Herzegovina), the intrusiveness of government control was felt to border on micro-management at the institutional level. This includes its approval of any changes in university organisation, but also impinges on faculty prerogatives with their overview and approval of degree programmes. This applies to Thessaly too, where the ministry of education has large impact because of control of budgets. At Skopje the national government appoints most board members. At Tavrichesky National, the government plays a large role through its education legislation and its approval of appointments. At Ankara, government control is also extensive; new curriculum proposals go through a review at the Turkish Council of Higher Education (YÖK) for approval. But in terms of its ability to foster democratisation and civic responsibility, the Turkish case suggests that the nation's stage of social and economic development may require a stronger government role initially. In Turkey, a high degree of government involvement has stimulated change in higher education because of its interest in expanding its links with the European Union. This has led to mandatory new education and training programmes in citizenship and human rights and on democracy. This may be an instance where top-down leadership accelerates changes to promote democracy and civic education.

A more moderate role for government was reported at Biccoca, where new governance structures have been implemented with the education ministry playing less of a role in administration. At Bergen, while the legal status of the university is controlled at the national level, a reform movement has produced recommendations for transferring more authority to universities by re-incorporating them as private or semi-private entities. Queen's University, Belfast's reliance on its government-funding base is changing as it was mandated to begin fulfilling its requirements through new sources of revenues.

Decision-making and accountability

Most institutions covered in this study reported that university administrations continued to maintain significant autonomy in decision making, often in spite of provisions for public hearings, solicitation of input and public reporting of decisions. Throughout the cases studied, it was almost universally reported that custom and practice, rooted in cultural traditions regarding social roles, supersede formal provisions and other attempts at expanding participation in university governance. At Tirana, past practices determine current institutional inertia as the management of the university continues to have a tendency to centralise and monopolise issues. Historically, the role of the government was pervasive and controlling through control of the budget. Now, Tirana and other universities are being granted increasing autonomy and have increasing discretion in the use of funds. As a result there are growing demands making transparency an increasingly important issue in university governance and decision making. Decision making at the top in many universities is generally not open to public scrutiny.

There is a strongly generalised perception among faculty and students across all institutions that a small group makes most decisions. Open systems, with full (voting) participation and procedures can have an indirect educational effect of promoting democratic practices and attitudes throughout the university.

Tuzla reported that a majority of those interviewed consider decision making as much too concentrated. Meetings are rarely open to the public. When there are public meetings they are usually connected with ceremonial or commemorative activities. The university communicates its decisions through public channels in the media. The representation of students on the University Council of Academic Staff is considered by the administration as sufficient input into university decision making. At Ankara, transparency and accountability are not really raised as issues as there is "an appearance of ...conformity between faculty, staff and students" to trust in decisions even though they do not participate in the process. At Tavrichesky National, self-censorship prevails with little discussion or debate on decisions. The tradition of hierarchical authority with no faculty participation in governance shapes current practice. Only department heads participate in decisions.

Thessaly also reported a lack of transparency in university governance, especially regarding financial matters. The Ministry of Education determines not only the amount of financial support, but also the pace at which it is allocated, making planning difficult. The faculty were more generous than students in their assessment of transparency in university decision making – a finding that was true on most issues across all the sites. However, a lack of knowledge affects the workings of formal structures too. The university community (faculty, technical and administrative staff and students) often do not have sufficient information or understanding of how governance works. For example, at Thessaly, faculty appointments, though occurring in a review process, are not transparent in their procedures.

One could also generalise from what was reported at Biccoca. Students tend to show indifference or ignorance of the decision-making process and do not concern themselves with university decision making. Student representatives themselves do not make use of official communication mechanisms, but rely more on "informal talks with faculty, other students and staff" to gather information and communicate their interests. At the university level, communication of decisions is inefficient. While deliberative bodies record their actions in public documents they are not easily accessible, with delays in the publication of the documents following the decision.

The evaluation of the degree of openness in decision making at Vytauti Magni is mixed. On the one hand, the perception is that few think that university decision making has become more transparent in recent years. However, a majority also believes that there is "satisfactory means available within the campus community to hold decision makers accountable for their actions".[74] There is also a perception of increasing openness in decision making. However, a majority of faculty believe that the administration is generally restrictive in its sharing of information about its decision making. This increases as decisions move away from academic matters to fiscal matters.

Samara appears to have changed enough in the past 10 years that the perception of greater openness and transparency exists. More faculty members sense that resource-allocation decisions are also being made on a fair and equitable basis. Decision making, however, is still concentrated in the hands of a few: "…student participation in university governance yields a contradictory picture. On the one hand, students take little part in decision making or do not take part at all. On the other hand, the university administration tries to improve their participation".[75] This seems to be fairly universal and is one of the ironies of participation in university governance throughout the reports.

An interesting contrast between formal arrangements to promote accountability and transparency and actual practice is highlighted by Queen's University, Belfast. A tradition of collegiality plays as much a role in fostering openness of decision making and accountability as do the organisational structure and statutory provisions. There is a long history of faculty and students having regular input into decision-making processes and consequently there is more of a consensus regarding transparency and accountability.

Surprisingly, given its long experience and democratic traditions, Bergen reported that most in the university community do not believe that the university has become more open and transparent in recent years. This raises some important questions. Is the degree to which the university community perceives decision making to be open and transparent relative to the historical and current socio-political environment? Are countries who are "more democratic" more likely to hold a higher standard of openness and

---

[74] Ibid., University of Vytauti Magni, Lithuania report, p. 85.
[75] Ibid., University of Samara, Russian report, p. 99.

transparency than undemocratic or transitional societies? Also, are there limits to the amount of openness and transparency a university administration can have? How does an institution know when it is doing a good job in this regard? The issue turns on the classic tradeoff between efficiency and equity. No university can be truly democratic because of organisational and management demands and because there are not unlimited resources to be applied to meet the needs of all faculty and students and the university mission. The goal must be the appropriate balance between the two. One of the special challenges to advancing the notion of universities as sites of citizenship will be to find ways to resolve the equity (democratic participation) versus efficiency (management requirements) tradeoff within the particular cultural and social circumstances in each national setting.

Tolerance, dissent and minority viewpoints

It is difficult to generalise or compare the sites on the extent to which they exhibited tolerance for dissent and minority or unpopular views. Most left it to inference, or made reference to constitutional or statutory provisions as evidence for this. Again, a brief inventory reveals the range of sentiment expressed.

Tirana does not offer a public forum for debate or discussion of different political views and questions. This may seem a bit ironic following its revolution and the opening up of society. However, we should not be too quick to judge university performance on these issues without some reference to time and circumstance. Is this position restricting political debate a backlash against former abuses and misuses of the university and the teaching function? Is it an immediate response to regulate or exclude political speech by elevating civil harmony over political debate? (Tirana is in the process of developing new courses and has attempted to introduce "proper" political studies to reflect more pluralism.) At the same time, no groups exist with the explicit purpose of promoting democracy. Also, few in the university community are interested in engaging in political activities outside the university. There has also been more emphasis on social engagement over political engagement. According to the site researcher, this is a reflection of the general weariness of the populace in engaging in politics. This may be the result of strenuous efforts to bring revolution and change. It could also be because in a period of post-democratic euphoria, attention is turning to practical needs such as jobs, economy, and training for such.

An overriding question seems to emerge from site reports as a whole: is there a danger of "democratic fatigue" in the newly independent countries and transitional societies?

The situation is different at many other sites. At Biccoca there is a good deal of conformity and low visibility of non-mainstream views. There are few student movements, and where there are, only a minority of students are involved in specific projects of interest to them. While "dissenting views can be expressed publicly" at the university and there is a "formal respect for processes", there is a belief that these processes are not always employed.[76]

At Vytauti Magni most students are aware of the existence of procedural mechanisms for the expression of views, but do not take full advantage of these channels. Differing viewpoints are not widely supported, in part because it is a very homogeneous country. It does have significant Polish and Russian minorities, however, and the Poles are demanding instruction in Polish in certain universities. Historical circumstances (instruction was at one time in Polish and the university renamed for a Pole) create the conditions for possible future conflicts.

Reluctance to engage in political debate was also reported at Samara. Students there go out of their way to avoid any discussion of ethnic and political conflict.

Community relations

Campus environments

How does this physical presence and infrastructure of the university affect its relationship with the community in which it is situated? Does the dispersal of university buildings and structures throughout a city increase the autonomy of its units and inhibit interaction with other faculty and students? Do residential campuses have a different relationship with their community than non-residential campuses where students and faculty conduct lives separate from the university? What makes the existence of a university in a community an asset to some and a source of conflict and tension to others? Such considerations affect both the development of communities within the university itself, and also the wider university-community relations.

At Tuzla the buildings and faculties of the university, including the student centre, are scattered around the city. Likewise, at Cergy-Pontoise sites are scattered, each of them cut off from each other. So, ironically, at Cergy-Pontoise, there may be integration of each site with the community in which it resides rather than with other university units. There is no sense of a unified campus since "each site has a tendency to exist independently from each other".[77]

Student housing is often the most significant issue in university-community relations and the clearest point of contact in non-campus based universities that may be dispersed across a community or city (Tuzla, Cergy-Pontoise). Such environments produce dispersed student populations and result in a fragmentation of student activities that are not university based, and inhibit the possibility of students coalescing around a particular set of issues. Such dispersal and fragmentation raise fundamental questions about how we are

---

[76] Ibid., University of Milan-Biccoca, Italy report, p.73.
[77] Ibid., University of Cergy-Pontoise, France report, p. 41.

to define and understand "community". Geography and local conditions are important to the number and nature of student-association activities and community engagement. Cergy-Pontoise and the local government all invest in the community in ways that are not directly apparent to the students who partake of services in the community.

At Biccoca there is no clear distinction between the university and the local community on most issues. "University and local community are not so distinct entities."[78] [sic] The researcher could not sort out the distinctions and issues over which the community and university interact. The issue was seen as pervasive and complex.

Student-community relations

In Thessaly, student-community relations have broken down to the point of hostility. It is unclear why, but the reports suggest that this is rooted in the government's decision to locate the university there to "revive" the local economy, which has resulted in class tensions in spite of the university's efforts at joint projects with the community and community education initiatives for the local populace. Community leaders, however, considered the university's involvement and investment in the town as vital to its future, and hoped that university traditions in democratic governance and civic engagement would "percolate down" to the local community.

In Tuzla, there is a strong political self-consciousness among students to work and interact in the community where they live. This may perhaps be part of survival strategy in the heightened nationalism following the war. Those interviewed believed that such participation in the community "advances civic consciousness, promotes democratic attitudes, [and] encourages political participation…".[79] On the other hand, it also provides proof of the old adage "familiarity breeds contempt", because some reported that as a consequence of these experiences in the community and the social and political world outside the university, apathy and political cynicism have increased.

At Cergy-Pontoise, students are not seen as students per se, but as members of the community in which they live through their associations in the area in which they reside. There is a dichotomy between a student's life as a member of the university and as a community resident. Students are very active in providing services for the community; however, the site researcher summarised these activities as "unfocused" and "sporadic". In Thessaly, although opportunities exist for such activities, the majority of students are not interested in community service or community work. Vocational interests dominate their thinking.

Meanwhile, at Biccoca there is a reliance on formal structures. Student relations with the local community are managed through liaisons with

---

[78] Ibid., University of Milano-Biccoca, Italy report, p. 76.
[79] Ibid., University of Tuzla, Bosnia and Herzegovnia report, p. 34.

government organs. This may reveal some problems with conceptualisation, development and implementation of programmes for democracy education and civic engagement and their evaluation. How are we to discriminate student and faculty roles as such from their role as citizens and residents of the community? If we are going to promote the notion that universities are, and can be, enhanced to be sites of citizenship, we will need a proper understanding of how to discriminate these varied roles that each individual brings to the university and the community in which they live.

Vytauti Magni presents a different case of a university town originally created to serve the university. Originally, a "student town" was formed in Soviet times that included housing, clubs, sports venues, shops, post offices, etc. With independence and privatisation reforms, the relationships between the local community and the students and university are now breaking up. This has created financial hardship for students and is beginning to affect their college-going behaviour and decisions on where to live. Because of this situation, students have a mixed view of the value of participation in community-based projects. They gain increased knowledge about real problems, but it also produces higher levels of cynicism and apathy.

In contrast, in Samara, students believe in voting in local elections but voting is seen as a personal duty, though many think the university should encourage it more. Students value their community-based projects highly. At Bergen, students are not encouraged to get involved in local politics or co-operate with the community on local problems. Queen's University, Belfast, in contrast, has long encouraged students to provide service to the community and has a student Community Action that facilitates student volunteerism in the community.

University-community relations

The Kosovo crisis in 1999 stimulated greater university-community co-operation at Tirana. Research projects and field experiences are now the main mechanisms for students to interact with the local community. However, "strained finances" limit the amount of support the university can give to such interactions with the community. There are two significant projects dealing with civics and democracy for undergraduates and in teacher training that specifically address this need. The local community's past access to university resources were limited by the isolation of the university, the lack of facilities and equipment, and "fear of mismanagement". Old animosities are in the process of being laid to rest so the university considers it important that it do nothing to exacerbate tensions in the community. Also, many previous relationships are tied up with conflicts associated with changes in 1990. Because some university property had been built on land seized by the state, current resolution of claims from an earlier era, along with privatisation of state property has rendered some of the university property unusable. Until new legal arrangements are promulgated and understood, the university sees a need to maintain harmonious relations with the community.

Meanwhile, in Tuzla, community residents have no access to university facilities. At Thessaly, however, part of its mission (as with Cergy-Pontoise) is to "reinvigorate" the community. The government located the university in the town to help develop the local economy and to address declining industrialisation of the town and region. Cergy-Pontoise saw the need for a student centre as an important addition to the infrastructure of the community. The University of Thessaly, meanwhile attempted to develop joint projects with the community, but the relationship is largely one of a "service provider" with community residents as "customers", so no true university-community partnership has emerged. Here again we see that the major impact a university can have on a community is in the development of infrastructure and physical establishment. There is also a great deal of friction between the university's faculty and students and the surrounding community. The university community does not feel its actions and outreach are reciprocated. Space and residency are big issues. Faculty did not settle in town. Some community residents are "unaware" of the university's existence. In this context the rector is trying to improve relations. Here again, we see an institution relying on personal relationships rather than institutional policies to address the university's relationship with the community.

The case of Samara reveals strong community relations through support for local government policy objectives with planning and expertise. Also, most people see the university as active in shaping the political and social life of the community but also see students as being less involved. The university has programmes in the community, but they are not designed specifically to increase student participation in the community. Skopje is an example of a relationship with the community that is strictly a consequence of the professional activities that go on in the university. The main points of contact with the community are through symposia, conferences and consultative relationships. Few volunteer activities occur and are not very representative of the university community as a whole.

In Bergen, the sentiment reported was that the administration does not do a good job of encouraging access to the university and its facilities by the local community. However, there is frequent contact between faculty and community representatives, but largely in their capacity as researchers and experts. The "university makes itself felt indirectly through its researchers".[80] This is a very common attitude and posture at almost all institutions.

Relationship with local government

A university's relations with local government can be qualitatively different from its relationships with the community and the residents themselves. Because of its history and the development of a university town within a town, Samara was extremely active and proactive in working with the local government. Much recent activity is tied to the transition to a market economy, democratic changes in society, and the university as a provider of

---

[80] Ibid., University of Bergen, Norway report, p. 117.

services and expertise required to facilitate transitions. The University of Tirana on the other hand, faces a major issue relating to privatisation of state property. Much university property is in limbo, and until legal issues are resolved, many facilities cannot be used. Bergen also does not actively support all the policy objectives of local government.

The nature of local linkages varies. Cergy-Pontoise's can be characterised as strong; others weaker or adversarial. What factors influence this? At Cergy-Pontoise, the university considers that one of its missions is to "bring life to the town". Here, as elsewhere, its biggest impact is on development and infrastructure and the physical structure of the community. This comes not only from the university's development of its own buildings, but the related development from the private sector to serve the intellectual and cultural interests of the university (restaurants, theatres, bookshops, etc.).

In Tuzla, the local community does not hold any functions or make use of university facilities for community events. As noted above, Tirana has no funding for community activities or programmes, with the exception of the community linkages directly related to national issues and Balkan crises; for example, much was done for Kosovo crisis support. The Tuzla research even went so far as to suggest that students would more likely do more in the community if they were paid for their work. This is perhaps not a surprise in an environment where volunteerism has not become institutionalised or expected among young people. Neither is there any tradition of activities such as fostering or advancing the student's career. Hence, Bosnian students see "no material reward" for civic engagement.

Another means of engagement with the community is through joint projects and by the solicitation of community experts and professionals to work with faculty or teach at the university. These activities also vary tremendously across sites. At Tuzla, community experts, though sought after in the past, are now prohibited from teaching. Formerly, "distinguished professionals" from outside the university were permitted to teach, but the new regulatory environment no longer allows this. Few are now invited onto campus to teach or provide guest-lectures.

Cergy-Pontoise on the other hand has very strong community support for the university and students. Local authorities have established consultative bodies on which students have representation. Though many are low profile and not major projects, both sides acknowledge co-operation and support from each other. Another instance of co-operation happens at Biccoca, which has established a consultative organ with representatives of the local government administration. Community residents – professionals and experts – are invited to teach and lecture through its operation.

At Vytauti Magni, the university actively participates in programmes and projects with the surrounding Kaunas municipality, including planning functions, providing research, and consultancies for the faculty. These professional relationships operate not just at the individual level but at the departmental level as well. The community can make use of university facilities at no charge. Similarly, the Samara faculty are also deeply involved in preparing programmes and training on problems of economic conversion, unemployment and training, and other labour issues.

Students and civil responsibility

Student life

University student unions mostly focus on student life issues: residential issues and housing (landlord relations), jobs, or cultural and educational values. At Tuzla, there was no feeling among the administration that it is the university's responsibility to provide more opportunities for students to engage in university life; it is seen as a student and personal matter. At Thessaly, however, students enjoy important social and economic rights (free tuition, textbooks, subsidies for housing and meals, plus medical care). However, these rights are circumscribed by underfunding, lack of fiscal autonomy and dependence on state funds under tight bureaucratic control.

At Bergen all students are members of the Norwegian Student Union that works to protect students' interests through universities and student welfare organisations. So too, the Ankara Student Union focuses mainly on the cultural and social life of students. The Vytauti Magni Student Union was resurrected following the model of student "corporations" that were active between world wars. These have been reintroduced to promote nationalism. Culture and sports clubs are very active and a primary focus of interest (as at Cergy-Pontoise, see below). It has an active political society for debates. Clubs and organisations are autonomous, without university regulation or overview.

Student clubs and activities were often affected by the wider society and the availability of resources. At Tuzla, even sports clubs could not be organised by the university. If students belong to one, they are in one organised by the community, town or canton. At Ankara, many clubs and extracurricular activities exist in the context of strong student autonomy and management of these organisations. Students are also independent financially and they alone are responsible for these organisations. Others such as Cergy-Pontoise provided funding for student activities such as these and have very elaborate programmes with much university support and large participation. Sports programmes are of particular significance and are conceived as being integral to the wider educational mission of the university.

Political societies for discussion and debate suffer not only from a lack of funding but a lack of interest. At Tirana, respondents claimed that "people are tired of engaging in politics", and that there is a trend on campus of stressing social engagement over political engagement. In contrast, at Vytauti Magni, the Political Science Club organises political discussions, especially before elections. However, few students think the university makes a serious effort to encourage students to get involved in politics and policy.

Biccoca presents a different picture. The only student groups that are self-managed are those with political or ideological orientations. They organise

111

as pressure groups in relation to university administration. Also, there are many extracurricular societies and clubs that students belong to that are completely outside university structures. Students belong to these as private citizens, not as students per se. Student life and roles are not defined by their membership in the student body. A student's identity is only partially formed by their role as a student and is fragmented because of their other outside interests. Therefore, it is not easy for the university to promote democratic attitudes as student interests go beyond participation in university governance.

Student representation

One generalisation that comes through all the site reports is that whether talking about university administration or student government, people believe that a small group of elites runs things. Each university, however, has different institutional and legal arrangements for participation in various university governance activities. Here again, an inventory of the variety of approaches to student participation in governance shows some similarities and differences between them.

In Tirana, because political parties are banned on campus, youth forums function independently from university structures and are a source of support for political parties. Also, ad hoc student clubs are self-organised by students for vocational purposes to lobby government agencies for jobs. There is no evidence of these activities taking on any degree of permanence yet. The site reporter noted rumours of students exploring new ways to organise themselves.

As noted above, the idea that elites run things was widely shared. Many sites reported that the same small group of student leaders always seemed to be involved in university activities or leadership roles. As a rule there was little participation and a general lack of interest among the student body as a whole. Some speculated that this was the result of a lack of maturity. Others posited the continuing problems of student life in acquiring housing, food, transport, and the other amenities of life to support their studies.

It seemed that the more active student bodies were those in the transitional countries or those that had experienced turmoil in the recent past (Vytauti Magni, Samara, Queen's University Belfast, Tavrichesky, etc.). Some have at least the perception of strong representation (Cergy-Pontoise, Vytauti Magni). Students feel the university is governed by democratic structures. However, in spite of a strong sense of democratic traditions, even in a young institution, students reported that this is often "more apparent than real" and that their role in governing bodies is minimised.[81] In consequence, there is low voter turnout for campus elections (about 10%).

---

[81] Ibid., University of Cergy-Pontoise, France report, p. 39.

At Thessaly, participation and voting in campus elections are in steady decline. However, governance structures allow student participation at all levels of decision making, including a substantial one-third membership.

What is the extent of their influence however? Why, with the level of statutory representation, is voting so low? Are they restricted on the issues they can vote on?

For such a large institution it seems odd that Biccoca has no student self-government. Students are, however, governed by and represented in the university's main academic bodies.

At Vytauti Magni the student union serves as one of the main governing bodies, with an elected presidium. Students participate in all levels of discussion with student representatives included in discussions on courses and programmes.

Samara has no sources of funds to help create and maintain new representational bodies. Students, therefore, are compelled to be more active among themselves. However, student government is seen as ineffective. Perceptions are that only a few students run things and many students feel excluded from participation in university life. Little is understood or known about the work and activities of student leaders and students as a whole are passive about it.

Bergen students are represented on all levels of governing bodies, which have dual administrative appointments for faculty and administrators. Students serve on the main university governing board and are elected in a politicised process, representing different political groupings. Still, the feeling is that a small elite dominates student opinion. Students likewise believe the university is run by a small group of people.

At Skopje the student union has branches in each faculty. However, the student body is very disorganised and "is the reason for the increasing abstinence of students from voting…and is at the same time an excellent indicator for the (un) popularity [sic] of the student organisation within the student circles".[82] Most students reported that the student union does not represent the interests of most students.

Tavrichesky National reported low participation of students in the management of the university. Students were nearly unanimous in claiming that the university does not consult with students. Neither do they have input into the curriculum. However, students have a high participation rate in the governance of their own organisations. Most think the student representatives do represent their interests. Faculty and administrators see student government as ineffective.

What can explain these differences? Do students exaggerate their influence and effectiveness among themselves (student organisations to student

---

[82] Ibid., University of Skopje, "the former Yugoslav Republic of Macedonia" report, p. 124.

organisations) because they have absolutely no influence at the university level?

At Queen's University, Belfast, the student union is well developed and influential and represents the most highly developed environment for student self-governance and participation in university governance. The executive staff of students is given leave from their studies to do this work full-time. Student representatives serve on university committees and also manage all clubs, sports and student societies on campus. There are no restrictions on the formation of student clubs and organisations except those that are religious or political, which may not receive university funds. The importance of the student union in the development of civic consciousness and political awareness is manifested in its record as a source of community and national leaders in later years after graduation from the university.

These findings suggest that the problem of participation and also effectiveness of participation is rooted in perceptions and how they affect motivations for action. Do attributions of elitist structures inhibit greater participation and foster the mentality that students cannot influence decisions and processes?

Attitudes and perceptions

Europe and the United States share a common problem of excess vocationalism among students. This pilot study revealed repeatedly that vocational interests dominated students' attention. This is not surprising since one of the primary reasons for attending a university is to advance one's position and ensure one's future welfare. Students are, and probably always will be, interested in acquiring good jobs and higher salaries. Therefore, it comes as no surprise that throughout the site reports, vocationally oriented and technical training programmes have the most influence on students' choices and behaviours.

Cergy-Pontoise reported the existence of bodies where students can voice their opinions, and that day-to-day dialogues between faculty and students are "complementary aspects" for students to learn and understand democratic structures and "were constantly mentioned by those interviewed".[83] Students there expressed little interest in social problems. Also, "increasing individualism results in low participation in communal activities".[84]

Students at Thessaly "insisted" that civic responsibility is best developed through personal and social relationships. In this view, there is no role for the university except indirectly through the student's interactions: "it is not a course's subject matter but the tutor's attitude that encourages civic responsibility".[85]

---

[83] Ibid., University of Cergy-Pontoise, France report, p. 39.
[84] Ibid., University of Cergy-Pontoise, France report, p. 43.
[85] Ibid., University of Thessaly, Greece report, p. 56.

Collegial governance was attributed to Biccoca, where many layers of organisation allow many channels for expression of viewpoints. While there are no prohibitions or obstacles to the expression of unpopular views, they are not encouraged either. History and culture dominate, as well as socialisation to a set of expectations on how things work. This is reflected in the notion that respondents reported "difficulties in reconstructing debates and processes that produced decisions".[86] There was much apathy towards specific political participation or involvement in governance processes, though "issues of the day" do engage people within the university.

At Samara, students have organisations for sponsoring political events and claim that the ability to espouse different views on campus is adequate. However, with weak student government and little participation in university governance, there is a sense of missed opportunities for citizenship education. Students, however, do not consider it a responsibility of the university to teach civic duties. This sentiment is echoed across the border in Lithuania where at Vytauti Magni only 25% see civic responsibility as a function of the university.

The report on Skopje revealed that despite weak governance and participation structures, and a long history of faculty autonomy and student inefficacy, most students surveyed thought the future of democratic society depended upon democratically educated students.

This suggests that the future orientation of students should also be considered in evaluating democratic attitudes and civic responsibility. If universities provide positive experiences in student interactions with university structures and with education programmes, the socialisation of students to democratic attitudes and a sense of civic responsibility may occur without it manifesting itself immediately in student behaviours during their years as a student.

Student rights

Students enjoy certain rights that vary by institution and country. But in all cases in this study it was clear that there was a real distinction between the de jure establishment and provision for student rights, and the de facto enforcement and protection of those rights. And, as with the other issues covered in this report, student, faculty and administration perceptions differ tremendously on the extent and effectiveness of these rights as well as students' knowledge and understanding of them.

At Tirana student participation is affected by general passivity, especially with regard to the assertion of their rights. Parents, it appears, are more likely to advocate a student's rights than the student her/himself.

---

[86] Ibid., University of Milan-Biccoca, Italy report, p. 73.

The importance of local political history in shaping attitudes long after events is suggested by the Thessaly report, which noted that earlier campus struggles in the 1960s were influenced by other student revolts and protests occurring globally. Those events helped to create much of the governance structure and rights available to students today. However, contemporary students seem to have little knowledge of this history and the struggle to advance and protect their rights and in consequence today "indifference and apathy are ripe".[87]

The availability of information about student rights was generally lacking at most institutions. Biccoca has no publications specifically on students' rights. No documents are published that specify rights. But the university statute and "didactic rules" contain information relevant to students' rights. Frequent references are made to the Institute for Students' Right to Study, but this deals mostly with student life issues and living requirements (housing, medicine, food, etc.). Few students know what their rights are and they are passive in their relationship to the university. Most consider other students the primary source of information about their rights.

Perhaps ironically, given the reporting of high levels of participation by students, at Vytauti Magni there is a feeling that the university does not do enough to inform students of their rights. Eighty per cent of students learn about their rights from other students.[88] Most faculty and administrators perceive that good information and resources are available to help students understand their rights and how to access the procedural process for complaints.

Samara projects a more favourable view of a university informing students of their rights. (One cannot tell from the material presented if it is substantively correct or what student perceptions really are from the material available.) Students care about their rights but do not know how to realise them. The university does little to inform students of their rights and this is also perceived as such by the students. At Samara, as at most other institutions surveyed, students' knowledge of their rights generally comes from their peers.

Skopje noted that students are only partially informed about their rights. Apathy is pervasive. Students do not fight for or demand their rights. They learn mostly about their rights from university publications (not specific) and student newspapers and pamphlets (student to student). Most rights are perceived to be centred on the right to study based on the Law on Higher Education.

Ankara claims that information is widely disseminated and is based on the higher education law, which pertains to their rights to study. Students rely heavily on friends and informal channels to learn them.

---

[87] Ibid., University of Thessaly, Greece report, p. 55.
[88] Ibid., University of Vytauti-Magni, Lithuania report, p. 88.

The situation at Tavrichesky National also reflects views expressed through many of the site reports, noting that faculty and administrators see information on student rights as the student's responsibility. There is no source of information on student rights.

Ombudsman

Most universities in the study did not have an ombudsman's office; that is, an official university office that exists for processing student complaints, grievances or for enforcing the protection of student rights. None were reported at Tuzla, Tirana, Ankara, Biccoca, or Tavrichesky National. The lack of an ombudsman is particularly critical at institutions characterised by authoritarian management styles and contributes greatly to students' sense of inefficacy and helplessness.

At Biccoca, channels for complaints or grievances are vague with no established procedures. While complaints can go to the rector's office, they are normally reviewed at a lower level first, or they can go through student representatives and be officially presented to the university governing body. It is unclear how well this works.

However, here as elsewhere at the sites studied, there seems to be powerful socialisation influences at work in terms of the expectations students and faculty have about mediating conflict or resolving disputes. That is not to say that they are democratic or otherwise. Student passivity and universal declarations of inefficacy with regard to university governance and processes suggests that the socialisation that does occur is marked by futility. Expectations are, therefore, low. This should not be interpreted to mean that the university community and students in particular are satisfied with the status quo – quite the contrary; it may mean that students are simply resigned to being unable to alter or influence decisions and policies that directly affect them.

Tirana noted that employees at all levels lacked employment security and had no office or mechanism for employees to deal with situations that threatened their position. The administration there can be arbitrary in hiring and dismissals. There is no unionisation. However, proposed revisions of the law may bring change: a new Ombudsman Law and Civil Service Law are beginning to create the conditions for legal protection for those with unpopular views or dissenting opinions.

Biccoca reported that it had no special office to protect those expressing unpopular views. However, there is statutory protection, and according to the site researcher, the absence of an ombudsman's office does not appear to inhibit the expression of dissenting viewpoints.

Unusual among the transitional states, Vytauti Magni has two offices ("commissions") for review of conflicts and ethics and a rectorate-level office for further review. Samara also reported having an ombudsman and institutional resources for students to access due process if they are accused of a wrongdoing.

Tirana also reported that it had no procedures for processing complaints and no ombudsman. The researcher noted that the "lack of procedures creates confusion". Tirana offers students no right of appeal, nor protection against arbitrary decisions. In consequence, students rarely file complaints because of the perceived futility of doing so.

It appears that part of the problem at many of these institutions is rooted in a communist or authoritarian legacy. Hierarchical structures and centralised planning and decision making did not allow for such channels. Even with more theoretical openness, students do not know where to begin to look for more information on the extent of and means of protecting their rights. There is still an internalised distinction between private and public expression of issues and concerns.

Early socialisation, combined with this legacy and the continuing structures and institutional inertia, is a limitation on the extent to which changes and more openness have affected perceptions about process, students' knowledge and the available actions open to them.

Funding issues

Funding for expansion of programmes and instruction in human rights, law, and democratic institutions is an issue at the sites surveyed now and will be so in the future. Existing structures and budgets in many countries, especially those less well endowed or those recently wracked by conflict or war, are barely sufficient to maintain existing programmes. Outside funds have been the catalyst in several instances for new classes, student research projects, or faculty leave-time for the pursuit of community-related projects and research. Currently, little funding is available at many institutions for student activities such as clubs, sports, and various intellectual and professional societies. Some institutions have funds only for specific and narrowly defined projects.

Democratic pedagogy and promotion of civic engagement

Reliance on societal norms

Many sites reported that university faculty and administrators had no expectations to advocate democracy or civic responsibility. Many thought that civic responsibility cannot be taught and there is a general lack of encouragement by the university to do so. Likewise, many expressed the sentiment that such a requirement may be at odds with the primary mission of the university, which is to provide training and specialist knowledge. Few institutions seemed committed to really pushing a democratic or civic engagement agenda. Participation in community and other civic engagement activities is seen by many as interfering with the educational mission.

This was the case at Tirana, where the promotion of civic responsibility and engagement is not perceived by students as an objective of the university. The record is unclear on the university's efforts to co-operate in providing new or additional information on these matters. The belief was expressed that good citizenship would "trickle down" to the community and to students only by the example the university and its faculty and non-teaching staff sets.

Likewise, Cergy-Pontoise reported that much education in democracy comes from the day-to-day contact individuals have with authority structures and university and community leadership. This view suggests that education for democracy is received through the daily, personal experiences students have in their life.

We should not underestimate the meaning or effect of these perspectives. Nor should those who want to see democracy and civic education placed at the centre of the educational mission of universities be critical of those institutions that reported, as many did, that so much of what passes for civic engagement and democratic participation is considered the individual's responsibility. This view challenges the notion at the heart of this study that universities are important sites of citizenship. But we must not beg the question that this view speaks to by ignoring the important and fundamental societal context in which universities operate.

Organisation for these tasks in the university

Most institutions reported a need for centres or institutes for the study of democracy, human rights or civic responsibility, but most also did not have such centres as planning or funding priorities. Some that did had established them as a response to external stimuli; for example, development of programmes in human rights, European institutions, and law as response to Tempus and Erasmus[89] and a desire to broaden connections with the European Union. Funds from private foundations and diaspora groups also facilitated such centres and programmes.

Nevertheless, many faculty and staff interviewed thought that learning about democracy and one's civic duties was realised indirectly through contact and experience with authorities and authority structures within the university. At Tuzla, for example, there are no programmes at the university that promote an understanding of civic duties and responsibilities. This site also was reported as considering such activities as a "watering down" of academic

---

[89] Erasmus is the higher education part of the European Union Socrates programme. The programme aims to support the European activities of higher education institutions and to promote the mobility and exchange of their teaching staff and students. The programme currently encompasses the twenty-five member countries of the European Union, the three members of the European Economic Area and two accession countries (Bulgaria and Romania). For further information, see http://europa.eu.int/comm/education/programmes/socrates/erasumus/general_en.html. Tempus is a European Union co-operation programme in higher education with non-EU members encompassing three broad areas: eastern Europe and central Asia (Tempus-Tacis), the western Balkans (Tempus-Cards) and the Mediterranean (Tempus-MEDA). For further details, see http://www.etf.eu.int/tempus.nsf

programmes by taking students' time away from their "regular" studies. In these cases, activities to promote civic engagement are seen as interfering with the primary educational mission of the university.

Many institutions thought that contributions in this area could be best made by social scientists and those in the humanities, since other faculties (in sciences and business) would not be concerned with a mission to educate for democracy. Such views are further tempered by the absence of official support for such objectives. Biccoca, for example, made no explicit reference to the promotion of democracy or citizenship in official documents or statutes. The university statute refers to the university mission as "cultural renewal through research and transmission of this information through education of the student". Students are free to act, but are not encouraged to do so.

At Bergen it was noted that the university held the belief that it should be a centre of learning that should foster certain values. However, increasing instrumentality and specialisation of expertise in education of students pose challenges to this mission. At Bergen, "the university leadership is not very specific about what it means by 'democracy', let alone 'true democracy', although it emphasises the necessities of cultivating an understanding of the complexity of society and balancing 'instrumental rationality' with 'intellectualising power' through education and personal guidance".[90] This comment perhaps best captures the indirect influences the university exerts on education for democracy.

Lack of money again was cited as an obstacle to the creation of new programmes for democracy education. Because of the lack of financial support for teaching staff interested in democracy and civic education at many institutions, they naturally gravitate toward external agencies and groups, for example, NGOs.

Evaluations

One means for students to participate in their education and in development of university curricula and policies is through the evaluation of courses, teaching staff and activities. The use of evaluations at the sites studied is not widespread, nor connected philosophically to the educational mission of the university, let alone to the wider question of their role in democratic citizenship. Sites can be split into four groups in their use of evaluations: those that do not use them and believe that students are not competent to judge academic matters; those that do, but do not take them seriously; those that use them and see them as important and effective; and those that use them only to meet official requirements, but ignore them. Without strong institutional support, evaluations will have no impact on the curriculum or the quality of teaching because students avoid negative comments for fear of reprisal in their grading. Evaluations must also be used without fear of

---

[90] Ibid., University of Bergen, Norway report, p. 114.

pressure from the administration or being the sole means of evaluating a teacher's effectiveness.

Classes and teaching

Most sites reported that their university did a good job of teaching for democracy and civic education, though most did so indirectly though courses in departments that would address the relevant subject matter.

Citizenship was approached in Bosnia with the expectation that universities will begin making more explicit statements about the acquisition of citizenship skills and responsibilities as part of their educational process. At Tirana, effort seems focused mainly on the social sciences and humanities and not the hard sciences. Structural factors critically affect the ability to place students at the centre of the learning process. Lack of teaching materials, overcrowded lecture rooms, and excessive teaching loads all contribute to the problem. More deeply ingrained problems are the deep-rooted traditions embedded in teachers' habits and approaches.

As noted, many universities thought that they addressed issues of democracy and civic responsibility indirectly; for example, in related courses, or in subject matter that implicitly deals with it. Tuzla sees this as being accomplished through incidental and indirect linkages to the community through class projects, field research, faculty connections and assignments. However, little is directly taught on key issues, which were "implicitly dealt with" – the exception being a course on democracy run by the journalism school.

The view that citizenship education is the responsibility of the student, acquired through indirect learning and personal experiences was reiterated by many. This perspective concluded that while students are exposed to concepts of pluralism, democracy, civil rights, political participation and political psychology, in classes they took, it was in the students' capacity as "citizens themselves" who are "most qualified" to set and define needs and priorities of community and society. Only after that should government, universities and other social and private organisations get involved. This view represents a major obstacle to advancing the notion of universities as sites of citizenship and will require special attention in subsequent research and in any discussions of curricular reform.

Cergy-Pontoise also considered much instruction in these issues to be "implicitly" acquired in the course of regular instruction in subjects that may touch on issues of democracy and democratic theory. Certain subjects and disciplines were more given to comparative study of society. Pedagogy was seen as important; that the correct teaching methods would also provide a means of acquiring democratic learning. However, many faculty members see the role of the lecturer as dispensing knowledge or communication of the subject matter that should be value-free. The findings from Biccoca echoed this belief and considered that certain established departments such as law and sociology would explicitly address issues of democracy in their courses.

Each institution repeated the general idea that their coverage of the subject matter on democracy and civic responsibility could be found in related subjects. While there were different emphases, each made similar points.

At Vytauti Magni there was a very vocational orientation. Because of the state of the economy and students' concerns about their future, humanities, philosophy and democratic and civic education are considered a luxury. However, it was also reported that most students could identify courses that explicitly address democracy or civic responsibility. Samara had few courses involving democracy or civic education, and no courses explicitly focused on these topics. Here too the subject matter is acquired indirectly from the curriculum. However, the university has developed special courses on elections and has an extensive field-based project for students to work in elections. At Ankara, instruction is in the related areas of civics, human rights and democracy, and is largely focused on pubic administration training programmes for public and private sector personnel to improve Turkish-European relations. Meanwhile at Bergen, most faculty members believed that while no courses dealing with civic responsibility existed explicitly, many courses indirectly broached the subject. Skopje also approached democracy taught within regular courses (indirectly) and in specific courses on democracy and citizenship in the faculty of law. Pluralism, political participation, civic duties, etc., are taught in courses in the law and philosophy faculties.

Throughout the reports there was a tendency to see democratic education as residing in the humanities and social sciences, which have a "natural impulse" for democracy. At issue was whether the natural sciences and technical areas are unaware of centres and programmes to promote democracy on campus or simply not interested.

This raises philosophical and pedagogical issues. Also, what role do the researchers' reflections play in the application of ideas and principles being examined in this study? Many reported that faculty as a whole felt such value-laden subject matter was not within their purview or even that it got in the way of the primary instructional purpose. Many sites reported that the university always encouraged dialogue with the student community and had many mechanisms for explaining university objectives. Yet surveys reveal a strong dissonance. How are we to understand this? Each site responded differently and conceived it differently. It is important to have some functional comparisons of what counts – some measure that addresses the gap between what is available and what is actually communicated, processed and received by the students.

One thing most universities had in common were fairly well-developed activities to make use of the community for field-based research and projects. Field study and research were an important source of learning at many, if not most sites. However, growing numbers of students and rising student/faculty ratios may soon create a barrier to promoting independent study and directed field research experiences. Those that were not engaged as much were considering more "joint projects" between the university and the community. But in some instances this is really service and contract work for government agencies and not field-based research connected with classes. Academic programmes are not designed to specifically address students undertaking citizenship responsibilities after graduation. The main purpose of education is creation of specialist knowledge. Students are as much responsible for this perspective as the universities are that offer the courses. Students are utilitarian in their academic interests and are worried more about grades and later jobs.

It is unclear what the impact of field-based projects is in terms of better relations with the community or if it would increase the likelihood that students would subsequently vote in local elections. Experience to date shows a remarkably mercenary outlook with students suggesting that they would place more value on field research or community involvement if they received some kind of compensation for it or a grade.

One site (Biccoca) does not allow independent study and had no extracurricular activity devoted "even partially" to teaching citizenship. It reported that there is little evidence of democratic teaching methods and little apparent need for it given the passivity of students.

Vytauti Magni on the other hand noted that since independence, "more democratic" relationships are occurring between faculty and students and this seems to be the key to civic education there at this time. There are no specific courses but the articulated mission and purpose of the university strives to foster active citizenship. While it is not possible to evaluate the claim, the assertion was made there that communication, faculty-student interaction and more open systems and processes "reveal" or teach democracy to students; this reflects faculty sentiments throughout many of the site reports.

Multiculturalism

Most sites had a difficult time understanding and explaining multiculturalism and what the university was doing to address the issue. Language study was most often cited as the locus of most multicultural study and the best way to learn about other cultures. We must beware that language study, however essential it is, does not become merely a surrogate for real engagement of issues of understanding and conflict resolution.

Additional conclusions and considerations

One of the main issues in the reform of European higher education is how to resolve the problem of increasing and maintaining university autonomy while promoting changes to accommodate the European desire for greater mobility of students and staff, reform of degree structures, and promotion of greater interuniversity co-operation and collaboration. "Structural convergence" – the harmonisation of national and institutional policies and practices with pan-

European initiatives – seems to be both a logical necessity and outcome in addition to serving as a signpost for policy.[91]

In addition to the findings reported above, a few last issues gleaned from the site reports that did not fit into the discussion above, as well as some conceptual and philosophical issues must be commented upon. As a pilot study, the University as Site of Citizenship project does not seek to draw too many overarching conclusions. The data and information gathered from the surveys and reported in the monographs have begun the process of identifying appropriate indicators of civic engagement. It contributes to new ways of thinking about pedagogical responses to the problems of democracy and civic responsibility. The study also raised questions for further enquiry and pointed to dimensions of issues that the questionnaires did not adequately cover.

Foreign students

For example, the status of foreign students was not adequately addressed. While many sites did not have large numbers of foreign or international students, most also reported that the trend was growing. Some had large indigenous minority populations. So the issues surrounding international students and minorities will take on increasing salience in the near future. Though underplayed in the reports (largely because of lack of history and experience in dealing with these populations), universities will need to address the infrastructure requirements and student life services together with programmatic and procedural requirements to make these students full members of the university community.

Assessment of key terms

Many in the Contact Group reported that the administration of the survey stimulated thinking and debate in the university regarding the issues raised in the study. On the other hand, it appears that some questions were excessively salient in eliciting particular opinions, and seemed to have had a prescriptive bias. Researchers and respondents both faced the problem of interpretation of concepts and language, especially the most central concept to this study, "democracy". The term has many uses, including "participation", style of management, political discussion and free expression, or participation in elections. There seems to be a need for much better conceptual discrimination between "civic engagement", "democracy", and "political participation". There is too much of a tendency to equate them. One outcome of the pilot study will be the assessment of key terms for revision of questionnaires and research protocols. The interpretation problem raises questions about the extent to which tradeoffs are made and recognised in the coverage or extension of key concepts in terms of the

---

[91] Is there a danger in this if "structural convergence" also becomes a test of a university's progress towards reform?

range of phenomena they are meant to cover. Researchers also reported needing additional material and data to interpret the survey for respondents.

Individual versus pedagogical responsibility

The faculties surveyed constantly contested the idea that universities should stimulate democracy among students. This will pose unique challenges to implementing new programmes or pedagogies pertaining to democracy and civic education. One persistent question is the extent to which what is going on in the university is reflected and shaped by what is going on in the larger society. Some sites stressed that there is dialogue that goes on at different levels in the university, particularly at the faculty-student interaction level, that facilitates learning about civic responsibility and democracy. Does such "dialogue" substitute for purposeful democratic pedagogies? Do mechanisms for communication and input serve as a surrogate for direct participation and voting in governance processes? Is there some minimal level of dialogue that allays the concerns of students and faculty that their voices are being heard?

Is it possible that the locus of democratic development and civic engagement for students is in the number and quality of extracurricular activities a student participates in? In the absence of explicit teaching in democratic principles and civic responsibility, such activities take on special importance. The reports suggest as much in the repeated emphasis by respondents and researchers on the individual's own responsibility and initiatives for greater involvement.

Broader philosophical issues and reflections

Is the university merely a reflection of the larger society? As Jean-Marie Imhoff who represented the University of Cergy-Pontoise in this project, noted, "it seems that the more democratic the society, the lower the participation rate". The central research question this poses is whether this is true only in the specific or isolated case, or if it is true in a broader, more generalised, cross-national context. What is in the developmental dynamic of democracies that produces this? Does it represent collective psychological and attitudinal atrophy – a societal hardening of the arteries of older democracies?

Each country represented in this study is at a different developmental level characterised by different levels of maturity of democratic institutions and processes and the maturity of reinforcing social norms and democratic political institutions. Experience, beliefs, and socialisation processes will be different in each society; not only for idiosyncratic cultural and historical reasons, but also because of the quality of and access to democratic institutions and processes. Will purposeful, integrated educational programmes for civic engagement accelerate the developmental dynamic of democracy?

There are structural conditions that may produce some of the effects we have witnessed in these studies. The time that students spend in university is relatively short. Students are "passing through" and may naturally be more focused on their personal needs than those of society or the community. One institution is considering giving credit for students who serve in some representative capacity; that is, attaching some reward or utility to the service as an incentive to increase participation, or at least make the commitments to such service more meaningful.

There is an absence of awareness among students of belonging to a larger community. The French report states this succinctly:

> "Paradoxically, the freedom existing at the university appears to be a brake on involvement in the task of representative [sic]: the advantage of an absence of constraints is not compensated for by the indirect and rarely apparent benefits of serving as an elected representative." [92]

So, few students volunteer their time in this capacity.

There is also the matter of salience. Barring a crisis, what is the motivation for students and faculty to demand greater participation in governance and in accepting the demands of democratic responsibility and greater civic engagement? Does satisfaction produce as much apathy and non-involvement as cynicism? This could be a major obstacle to teaching democracy and citizenship, because of the overwhelming need to meet the vocational interests of students and ensure employment and relevant work. How can one inculcate democracy, civic values without some foundation of stability in sound social and political structures and reasonable expectations?

It may be that in certain countries, the socialisation of students to a new set of expectations regarding democracy and civic responsibility may be easier to execute than real changes in existing faculty, and technical and administrative staff attitudes. Authoritarian management styles create additional inertia inhibiting changes in organisational structures, curricula and teaching that would foster or create democratic values and practices. This suggests that the promotion of democratic values and civil responsibility is not merely a pedagogical question, but must also be addressed structurally in terms of the organisation and practice of university governance.

Many researchers were torn between reporting what they learned and what they believed. In some cases there was a clear dissonance between what was reported by the informants or what the university claimed to do, and what the researcher's interpretations were. There were some marked contrasts between faculty and student views of the situation at their institution, for example, in one instance the researcher could conclude that the university suffers from a democratic deficit in its administrative decisions

---

[92] DGIV/EDU/HE (2000), University of Cergy-Pontoise, France report, p. 40.

and governance regulations, yet also conclude that the faculty sees university decision making as more open than the students would.

How do we address the problem of "passivity" among students? Apathy, disinterest and passiveness can come from many sources: conflicting life priorities, general satisfaction with life, a lack of knowledge, a sense of inefficacy – all in spite of the existence of formal channels for participation and numerous organisations to facilitate it.

The way forward

Comparative research provides a basis for clarifying the context in which universities operate. Cross-national research clearly shows the differences between countries with many private universities and those that are entirely publicly funded and governed. Such research provides the opportunity to discover new findings and to learn what works and what does not work from the experience of others.

The Contact Group's reports and the survey data clearly demonstrate that in the minds of the respondents there is a significant perception among students of what their universities are doing and not doing with regard to democratic practices, and democracy and civic education. In terms of the political socialisation of students these findings give a good indication that universities have a significant impact on what students are doing with regard to democratic participation and perceptions. There is strong preliminary evidence that suggests that universities can be differentiated on the several dimensions identified by the data. University policies and practices do make a difference and are evident in the perceptions of students and faculty. The results show that we can design efficient and informed instruments that can give a fairly accurate portrayal of how universities perform in various dimensions of what constitutes the civil and democratic university.

As a result of this research we now have:

- a means of introducing a dialogue with policy makers to discuss the issues covered in this report;
- an efficient, cross-national way to measure, with some confidence, universities' commitments to democratic practices, democracy and civic education, and student participation in these activities;[93]
- a means for extending the research globally.

The next steps for this work could include distribution of these findings, as well as the findings of the US study, to appropriate policy-making bodies of the Council of Europe and related organisations. Distribution of this report and the US findings could be presented jointly to a wide audience, including the US higher education NGOs sponsoring the US study and other related organisations. In the United States, this has already begun, in several

---

[93] It appears that thirty-five to forty questions will configure universities along the dimensions discussed in this study, which will allow a profile of the place of democracy in these institutions.

presentations at national academic conferences, and by the preparation of at least two distinct publications. Distribution to higher education organisations across the globe that have expressed interest in the study might also be considered. The findings of the European and US studies could serve as a centrepiece of a widely distributed monograph on Universities and Democracy that would include findings from other studies from the US, Europe, and perhaps other areas of the world.

A global conference sponsored by the Council of Europe and US NGOs on Universities as Sites of Citizenship and Democracy could be a possible step to pursue. The conference would discuss the results of the study and their implications for higher education and democracy over the next decade. The conference could focus on developing plans for future co-operation, including the sharing of information on best practices and developing strategies for promoting civic engagement and on-going educational reform.

Improvement of the survey instrument and expansion of the study to a larger pool of universities across Europe and the United States (and perhaps to other areas of the world) might be worth pursuing. A wider and deeper pool of participating universities would not only strengthen the findings, it would also extend the impact of the work to additional universities and societies. Recommendations based on an extensive study of this kind would have powerful impacts, helping higher education institutions and governmental organisations and NGOs to discuss and determine their responsibilities for civic education and democracy.

The student charter: an example of good practice from Moldova

Sergiu Musteață, Angela Garabagiu and Sjur Bergan

Background

Moldova gained its independence in 1991, as one of the countries emerging from the former Soviet Union. It is located in the south-eastern part of Europe, bordering on Romania and Ukraine. With a population of some 4.3 million, it is the most densely populated of the former Soviet republics. Approximately 65% of the population speak Romanian as their native language, while the corresponding figures for Ukrainian and Russian are 14% and 13% , respectively.[94] The capital, Chișinău, is the largest city by far, with a population of some 800 000.

Higher education in Moldova emerges from the system of the former Soviet Union. In addition to classical universities, Moldova has a number of highly specialised higher education institutions – some of which bear the name of universities – that offer a limited number of academic disciplines. The largest institution is Moldova State University with some 21 000 students and 800 teachers. Other large institutions are the Academy of Economic Studies of Moldova, the State Agrarian University, the Ion Creangă State Pedagogical University (5 661 students and 348 teachers), the N. Testimitanu State University of Medicine and Pharmacy, the Technical University of Moldova, the State University of Arts and the Free International University of Moldova. In all, Moldova has thirty-nine higher education institutions,[95] including twenty-four private universities, teaching in Romanian, Russian, Bulgarian, English and French.

Higher education in Moldova suffers severe financial constraints, which retricts the undertaking of expensive research or even maintaining basic equipment, obliges staff and students to seek income outside higher education and – along with the country's relative geographical and political isolation – limits the possibilities for international co-operation. On the other hand, some funds are available from other sources. To quote Lewis Purser:

> "It is true that official salaries are very low, with the result that many staff are obliged to seek supplementary sources of income, from both inside and outside higher education. Limited public resources are to a certain extent being compensated for by private resources, although of course these are also limited. Nevertheless, some

---

[94] According to a census carried out in the Soviet Union in 1989.
[95] "Higher Education in the Republic of Moldova", Stefan Tiron et al., Unesco-Cepes 2003, p.81, quoted by Lewis Purser in his report from the Council of Europe seminar on Higher Education Governance and Reform, Chișinău, 16-17 October 2003.

universities would appear to have access to relatively significant resources from private sources, especially from student fees."[96]

This leads us to one consequence of the financial restraints, which is that, in addition to the students whose places of study are financed through a grant from the Ministry of Education, higher education institutions may admit additional fee-paying students, who are supposed to cover the cost of their own education. These two categories of students are commonly referred to as "budget" and "non-budget" students, respectively. The categories are not unique to Moldova, as they are found in some other countries in central and eastern Europe, such as several countries of the former Yugoslavia, but the categories would be unfamiliar to a western European reader.

As in other parts of the Soviet Union, research was largely carried out within the Academy of Science, whereas universities were mainly conceived of as teaching institutions, and, in spite of considerable efforts by individual staff, present conditions make it possible to change this division of labour only slowly.

Most importantly, for the purposes of the present article, the recent Soviet heritage of higher education in Moldova implies that students were largely considered as recipients of established knowledge who were not encouraged to play a proactive role in their education or question received wisdom. The relationship between students and teachers was one of authority rather than collegiality.

The concept of a student charter

Higher education has at least four main purposes:

- preparation for the labour market;
- preparation for life as an active citizen in democratic society;
- personal development;
- development and maintenance of an advanced knowledge base.

While much of the current debate on higher education policies seems to focus on the first aspect, the present book is mainly concerned with the role of higher education in developing a democratic culture without which democratic institutions cannot function and democratic society will not come about. The concept of the university as a site of citizenship, developed in considerable detail in Frank Plantan's article in this book, is crucial in this context, because it emphasises the fact that democracy cannot simply be learned through theoretical study and research, however important these may be to developing our understanding of democracy. Democratic culture is developed through participation and practice. A higher education institution that sought to develop a democratic culture through its classroom teaching

---

[96] Lewis Purser, op. cit.

while sticking to non-democratic patterns in its governance and student-staff relations would be likely to fail in its goal.

In the Moldovan context, this is no small challenge, in the light of well over a generation of Soviet heritage. It would indeed be difficult to find any Moldovan teacher or student in the early 1990s who, based solely on the practice in his or her own country, would have had personal experience of a democratic university culture encouraging active participation and the asking of critical questions to the university leadership. Even the view that students have certain inalienable rights, and that these go beyond a right to attend lectures, was not widely adhered to, at least not at the official level.

This, then, is the context that makes the concept of a student charter in Moldova an unusual one, not to say a revolutionary one. As developed at the Ion Creangă State Pedagogical University in Chişinău, the student charter seeks to spell out and codify the rights, but also the obligations, of students at this institution. By extension, the charter also seeks to spell out these rights and obligations in general terms, adapted to the Moldovan context. With minor adaptation, the charter could therefore be taken up by other Moldovan institutions, and in the European context, it is interesting as an example of good practice. Parts of the student charter will be immediately recognisable to students, staff and higher education policy makers from other European countries, while other parts may need a word or two of explanation for those less familiar with the Moldovan context.

Elaborating the student charter

The initiative to draft a student charter at the Ion Creangă State Pedagogical University was taken in 2000 by the co-ordinators of the Moldovan Site of Democratic Citizenship (Dr Elena Prus and Dr Sergiu Musteaţă). The student charter was developed by the Site of Democratic Citizenship established within this university as a part of the Council of Europe's Education for Democratic Citizenship (EDC) project, and then put into effect with the support of the Council of Europe.

The Working Group for the first edition was composed of two university professors, Dr Elena Prus and Dr Sergiu Musteaţă, and some students: Vlad Manoil, Andrei Murahovschi, Maria Neagu, Diana Cibotaru, Andrei Vasilachi, Cristina Ciobanu and Lili Franţ. These students represented different university departments: history, foreign languages, philology. These were the most active members of the League of Students. In the space of a few months they prepared material for the charter. They collected legal documents referring to the rights and obligations of young people and documents issued by the Pedagogical University (where the administration of the university provided all the necessary documents), analysed them and selected the information on students' rights and obligations. With a degree of supervision and co-ordination by the professors leading the project, the students worked to elaborate the text of the charter, taking into consideration official documents. They kept the original expressions from the existing laws, showing the sources, and combined the individual articles into a coherent whole. One of the most serious problems was the access to information, as there is no database of legislation in the youth field, or in the field of education.

The draft of the charter was discussed with lawyers, teachers and representatives of a number of local NGOs, such as the Students' League, the National Association of Young Historians of Moldova and the Students' Trade Union. When the required changes had been introduced, the text was translated into English and French by the students and checked by the teachers. The EDC co-ordinators and the EDC division of the Council of Europe approved the final version of the charter for publication.

The second edition was prepared under the supervision of the same EDC co-ordinators and the majority of the students from the first Working Group. Among the new members of the Working Group one should mention Ira Rurac, Segiu Micu, Angela Şolcan, and Irina Rusu.

Adaptation of European standards to the local context

As we have seen, there were strong reasons in the Moldovan context to begin work on a student charter. At the same time, this work was also well situated within a European context provided by the Council of Europe project on Education for Democratic Citizenship (EDC). The Moldovan co-ordinators for this project, Elena Prus and Sergiu Musteaţă, were also key people in the elaboration of the student charter, and the work on the charter was included in one of the actions of the EDC project, namely that of Sites of Citizenship.

The Council of Europe set up the Education for Democratic Citizenship (EDC) project in 1997. In doing so, the governments of Europe stressed the importance of education for democratic citizenship. The objectives of this project were to identify skills, attitudes and values that both young people and adults need in order to become active citizens; to develop strategies, teaching and learning methods to help acquire the competences needed for democratic participation; and to promote good practice in this field. The Council of Europe identified a series of good practices in specific areas that could be recommended as examples of democratic participation. They are known as sites of citizenship.[97]

The sites of citizenship involve the management of democratic life. They are initiatives taken at various levels: schools, communities, workplaces, neighbourhoods, cities, and regions. These sites facilitate the active participation of specific groups (often those socially excluded) in their own personal and community development and in decision-making processes at all levels. Examples include: young people from disadvantaged neighbourhoods learning about their rights and responsibilities (France);

---

[97] See "Sites of Citizenship", Council of Europe brochure, and "Sites of Citizenship: Empowerment, Participation and Partnership", report by Liam Carey (Ireland) and Keith Forrester (United Kingdom), 2000, (DECS/EDU/CIT (99) 62 def. 2).

mediation structures between different communities (Bulgaria); local community development partnerships (Ireland); and a one-day Youth Parliament (Belgium).

The initial objective of the Moldovan Site of Citizenship was to develop an understanding of human rights and democratic citizenship education as a discipline in universities and as part of the curriculum in secondary schools. The discussions held with students, however, demonstrated the need to go further then the acquisition of knowledge about democratic citizenship. Students realised the importance of democratic participation and therefore launched the idea of defining ways of student participation in university life. The charter was supposed to raise students' awareness of their rights and responsibilities and also to help them experience democratic participation. Both the final product – the charter – and the process of its development and approval were important. The process of drafting the charter gave opportunities for students to express their views on how the university is run. It allowed them to have a voice on matters that are of great importance, not limited to their leisure, as was usually the case at most Moldovan universities. They learned about the existing legislative basis that regulates university life in Moldova, as well as the relevant decision-making processes.

The Council of Europe secretariat and experts assisted the co-ordinators of the Moldovan site in the organisation of seminars on Education for Democratic Citizenship and in the development of the charter. A series of seminars took place in 2000 and 2001. The Council also supported an exchange of experiences between the Moldovan site and other European universities through a project on Twinning of Sites of Citizenship in 2001.

One cannot overestimate the importance of this project. It is an excellent example of learning and practising democratic citizenship based on the values of human rights, equality, interdependence and accountability. The students of the Ion Creangă University developed knowledge of democracy, rights and responsibilities, the structure and function of institutions and intercultural relations. They acquired skills for democratic participation, such as problem solving, communication, discussion and dialogue, critical reflection, teamwork and co-operation. And, finally, they changed their attitudes by becoming more open to others, having a greater acceptance of cultural and social differences and respect for commonly agreed norms.

Today, democratic governance in education institutions is given great attention at various international meetings. The Council of Europe's Committee of Ministers states in Recommendation Rec(2002)12 [98] that acquisition of knowledge, attitudes, values and key competencies for democratic citizenship "should be encouraged: – through active participation of pupils, students, educational staff and parents in democratic management of the learning place, in particular, the educational institution". The Prague Forum and the Athens Ministerial Meeting in 2003 went further by stressing the importance of establishing criteria for good quality in education, one such

---

[98] Recommendation Rec(2002)12 of the Committee of Ministers to member states on education for democratic citizenship.

criteria being the presence of democratic processes in these institutions. Ministers of education requested the Council of Europe" to develop quality indicators and tools for self-evaluation and self-focused development for educational establishments, and to identify models of good practice in the areas of democratic governance and quality assurance … and prepare their potential users to be able to make use of them".[99]

Additional information on the EDC project may be found at http://www.coe.int/T/E/Cultural_Co-operation/education/E.D.C/.

The student charter: the issues

While the full text of the student charter is reproduced in Appendix 1, it may be worthwhile outlining the main issues addressed in the charter and putting them in their proper context.

Part 1

Chapter 1

In addition to giving some key definitions and underlining the applicability of definitions provided by other laws and regulations, such as that of a "student", defined as any person accepted for admission to a higher education institution, from the moment that decision has been made by the competent authority (Article 3), the first chapter of the first part of the charter spells out some issues of a general as well as a specific nature. It underlines the students' right to the recognition of their personality and, in language based on the European Convention on Human Rights and also used in the Council of Europe/Unesco Convention on the Recognition of Qualifications concerning Higher Education in the European Region (Lisbon Recognition Convention), unequivocally states the universal principle of non-discrimination. It is interesting to note that the charter specifically states that foreign students should have the same rights and obligations as Moldovan students.

Two issues are underlined with particular emphasis because of the recent history of Moldova and the composite character of its society. One concerns the recognition of a student's national culture and religious confession, while the other concerns the rights of a student to education in his/her own language at any level of education. This right is granted under the constitution of Moldova as well as under a specific law on the functioning of languages on the territory of the Republic of Moldova.

At the same time, the charter indicates that all students, regardless of their linguistic or other background as well as of their field of study, shall take an

---

[99] 21st session –"Intercultural education: managing diversity, strengthening democracy", Athens, Greece, 10-12 November 2003, Declaration by the European Ministers of Education on intercultural education in the new European context.

obligatory course in Romanian language and history. The obligation of higher education graduates to demonstrate a knowledge of Romanian reappears in Article 26, on the obligation of graduates, and reflects the sometimes heated discussions on the issue of the state language. Already in the first chapter, a certain balance between rights and obligation emerges, and this balance will be found throughout the charter.

Chapter 2

The second chapter covers a wide array of student rights and obligations, ranging from the right to freedom of expression and assembly through to the right to financial support if needed, and the right to an adequate living standard to the right to leisure. The rights outlined in this chapter could possibly be systematised as follows:

- democratic/political rights (expression, assembly, etc.);
- physical protection (Article 15);
- moral protection (Article 16, dignity and honour);
- legal and administrative rights (information, petition, right to appeal). These could also be considered as political rights, but they are outlined in the charter with specific reference to administrative bodies;
- social and economic rights, but as these constitute a quite prominent part of this chapter, it may be useful to divide these into:
  - the right to student support (in particular scholarships);
  - the right to employment;
  - the right to leisure;
  - the right to accessible medical care (Article 24);
- cultural/intellectual rights (Article 17);
- the right to fair recognition of foreign qualifications (Article 19), which is of course one of the key areas of the Bologna Process and also the subject of the Council of Europe/Unesco Recognition Convention.

Two further aspects of this chapter may be worth noting. First, while in some cases, it is clearly indicated who is responsible for implementing student rights; that is the higher education institutions, but also, for example, the Ministry of Health in the case of health care or simply "the state", as in the case of the right to leisure – this assertion is entirely absent in other cases, such as relating to the right to employment. It is interesting to note the particular emphasis, in Article 12, on the duty of "official sources" – a reasonable interpretation of which seems to be the competent authorities of the higher education institution – to provide students with adequate information on the life of the institution. This provision is clearly intended to remedy what has been perceived as a major problem in the Moldovan higher education system.

Second, while most of the articles are brief and mainly state the principle involved with relatively few details as to implementation, the right to scholarships is covered in great detail. In this sense, the charter shows traces of two distinct legislative traditions in Europe, where one relies on brief and general laws to be interpreted in an evolving context of policies, whereas the other relies on detailed legal prescription that leaves considerably less scope for a flexible interpretation.[100]

Finally, the second chapter includes two articles covering student obligations, which, in addition to the obligation to demonstrate knowledge of the state language already referred to, include the obligation to show respect for others as well as to abide by the relevant laws and regulations.

Chapter 3

The third chapter addresses the organisation of studies. Most of the articles specify students' rights with regard to their studies, and some spell out adaptations of the general rights described in Chapter 2 to the specific fields of studies. This is true, for example, of the right to appeal, which in Article 33 is specified to extend to the right to lodge an appeal against the outcome of an examination, and the right to fair recognition, which in Article 35 is extended to include the right of academic mobility and specified as the right to transfer between Moldovan and foreign higher education institutions.[101]

This chapter also states that students have the right to pursue two academic specialisations simultaneously as a part of their degree programme, a point which addresses a perceived lack of flexibility within the Moldovan higher education system and which would, in fact, bring it closer to what is emerging as a European standard through the Bologna Process. In this, as in some other areas, the charter distinguishes between budget and non-budget students. The latter pay study fees per programme or specialisation and may undertake a second specialisation only if they pay the corresponding fee. The chapter further covers the issue of "academic leave"; that is, the right of the student to break off their studies for good reason such as sickness, pregnancy or child care, without losing their study place, and it also addresses the right of part-time students in some detail.

Chapter 4

The fourth chapter addresses issues related to graduation and life after graduation, essentially employment. In this sense, it addresses the relationship between higher education and an important aspect of the society of which higher education is a part. The provisions relating to graduation essentially deal with the documentation of the graduate's achievement and make explicit reference to the Diploma Supplement elaborated by the European Commission, the Council of Europe and

---

[100] On this issue, with specific reference to higher education, see Sjur Bergan: "A Tale of Two Cultures in Higher Education Policies: the Rule of Law or an Excess of Legalism?", in the *Journal of Studies in International Education* – Volume 8, Issue 2, summer 2004.
[101] Fair recognition is, of course, a prerequisite for academic mobility.

Unesco, which parties to the Bologna Process have undertaken to issue to all students free of charge as of 2005. On the other hand, the provisions that students with two fields of specialisation within the same degree be issued two diplomas is at variance with prevailing standards elsewhere in Europe.

The provisions covering employment require a word of explanation as, to a western European reader, the provision that a budget student be obliged to work for a three-year period in the job to which they will be assigned by the Distribution Commission, and that, within this period of three years from graduation, they can seek a job on the free labour market only if they repay the cost of their studies or if the Distribution Commission fails to assign them a job, will undoubtedly raise some eyebrows. This is so even if the obligation on students to accept the assigned job is combined with an obligation on the relevant state authorities to provide such employment and to cover expenses if the employment entails a move.

These provisions must, however, be seen in the context partly of Moldova's past as well as the current difficult situation of the country. The notion of state service in return for a higher education covered by state funding was a part of the Soviet system. While it is not a part of the higher education tradition of western European countries, it is not unknown in other contexts, such as education provided by private companies, attendance of shorter, often expensive, courses provided by both public and private employers, or indeed certain kinds of public education, where the typical example would be that graduates of military academies are often bound to a given period of employment as officers in the armed forces following graduation. It is therefore not so much the principle of free education linked to a period of obligatory service that would raise questions, but rather its extension to all kinds of higher education. In the current situation in Moldova, with a very difficult economy and high unemployment, many graduates may also find that the restricted choice of initial employment may be offset by the obligation of the state to provide such employment as there is. Even if not ideal, such assigned jobs may be an attractive alternative to unemployment, if in fact the state is able to follow up on this obligation. The provision in Article 42.3 that "young specialists have the right to be provided with accommodation, electricity and fuel during the first three years of teaching" further underlines the dire situation of the country.

Chapter 5

Chapter 5 addresses the defence of students' rights and may largely be seen as a specification of the general right to free expression and assembly included in Chapter 1, with special reference to the activities of student organisations (in the charter referred to as "trade unions"). The principle of non-discrimination included in Chapter 1 is re-stated in Article 51, and the chapter also states the principles of presumption of innocence and the right of students accused of any offence to defend themselves against the accusations before a decision on possible sanctions is taken. Some provisions might give rise to questions from the point of view of standard European practice, in particular the obligation to "stop activities damaging to the trade union movement" and the obligation to "participate in the activities of the trade union institution". It is perhaps more the wording of these obligations and the need to include them explicitly that draws attention, rather than the principles themselves, although passive membership of organisations would seem to be more common than an active one in many countries, even if this is of course not ideal. Likewise, the injunction against corporal and violent punishment draws attention not because of the principle but because of the perceived need to include it.

Part 2

Chapter 1 of the second part of the charter establishes students' right to a place in university hostels, assigns the student organisation(s) a role in the selection of tenants and establishes a tenants' council, whereas Chapter 2 establishes the tenants' rights and obligations in considerable detail. Many of the provisions of this chapter could in fact have been included in the rules of the student hostel, but their inclusion in the charter may serve to underline that equal and transparent access to student housing is critical for many students given the economic problems of the country. Article 59, which provides for incentives for students that contribute to improving the conditions of the hostel, is well worth noting.

Part 3

This part addresses the specific situation of non-budget or fee-paying students. Chapter 1 specifies the rights of this group of students, whereas Chapter 2 specifies their obligations. Provisions in both chapters are largely of a contractual nature, but they also serve to underline that, apart from the fees and certain obligations on both the institution and the student that follow with payment, the status of non-budget students is not radically different from that of budget students. We are certainly not talking about two very different groups of students, where the payment of a fee opens the doors to privileged treatment and greater opportunities. In particular it is worth noting that Article 64 underlines that admission should be in accordance with the institution's regulations and be based on the student's qualifications. The students with the highest grades in the entrance examination are accepted for places of study free of charge, but fee-paying students also have to meet the minimum qualifications, so that places of study cannot be bought outright.

The student charter as an example of good practice

As we have seen, the student charter elaborated at the Ion Creangă State Pedagogical University covers a relatively wide array of topics. While some provisions are immediately understandable to most European students, staff and higher education policy makers regardless of their national and cultural background, other provisions can be explained only if the specific situation of Moldova is taken into account. Even then, there may be provisions in the charter that could be contested, but this should not detract from the fact that the elaboration of the charter is a considerable achievement. The charter is particularly remarkable in a country without a long-standing tradition of civil rights or, for that matter, student rights.

The charter contains a wide range of rights and obligations relating to various actors, and its force is moral rather than legal as, clearly, a student charter adopted by the Students' League of the Ion Creangă State Pedagogical University cannot be legally binding on actors such as the Distribution Commission and ministries (see the articles on employment) or for that matter decide on the organisation of studies, which in part comes under the auspices of the ministry of education or even, for some issues, under that of parliament.

The fact that the charter, while elaborated in the form of a legal document, is primarily a moral statement should, however, not diminish its value and importance. It is a very significant statement by a group of actors immediately concerned in the topic it covers: students and a group of reform-minded teachers. Its contents as well as its form make it a very valuable source for those in positions of appropriate authority who might wish to transform the provisions of the charter into binding legal obligations through modifications of the relevant rules and regulations. The balance between students' rights and obligations underlines the commitment of the students and will probably increase the credibility of the charter in the eyes of the authorities of both the university and the ministry while showing that students do not believe they have only rights without obligations. In the context in which the charter was adopted, this aspect is not to be underestimated.

From a wider European perspective, the charter combines universally accepted principles with adaptation to the local situation. This could be seen as a weakness by some, but we see it rather as a strength as long as the adaptation does not infringe on key universal principles and here, in our view, the student charter has managed to strike a reasonable balance. Europe is a unique balance between unity and diversity, between our common heritage and different traditions that have evolved on the basis of this common heritage. Not to adapt a document such as the student charter to local circumstances would, in our view, reduce its effectiveness, and we see this adaptation as a part of its role as an example of good practice.

From this wider European perspective, the student charter might have been phrased differently on certain points and, given that it takes the form if not the function of a legal document, it might have benefited from covering some of the issues in less detail. Nevertheless, it is, to our knowledge, a unique example of a charter of student rights and obligations elaborated on local initiative in a society and a higher education system emerging from a long tradition of top-down government and disregard for student rights. The local initiative addressed local conditions, but it did so within the European framework constituted by the European Convention on Human Rights, the Council of Europe project on Education for Democratic Citizenship with its attendant guidelines and text, as well as the current movement of higher education reform in Europe, embodied by the Bologna Process.

The student charter aims to turn the Ion Creangă State Pedagogical University into a true site of citizenship in which students and staff have a stake in the development of their institution in line with the values, standards and heritage of European society in general and European higher education in particular. The student charter deserves not only to be studied, but also to be emulated by others wishing to strike an appropriate balance between European standards and values and the particularities of local circumstances.

APPENDIX

The Moldovan Student Charter

Elaborated by a group of students and teachers at the Ion Creangă State Pedagogical University within the framework of the Council of Europe project on Education for Democratic Citizenship

Argument

Today's society requires changing people's mentality through education. More and more we need a new form of education – dynamic, formative and based on values. In this sense, university and school are the central factors in promoting change. On the other hand, lifelong learning and global education imply stressing the content rather than the objectives. We are witnessing an explosion of content by means of a new type of education: education for peace, education for change, education for intercultural dialogue, ecological education, etc. Being a part of this group, education for democratic citizenship requires an inter- or trans-disciplinary solution with implications for the whole educational system. These new types of education aim to prepare both the individual and the community for a conscious and responsible evaluation of a complex world.

The project Education for Democratic Citizenship (EDC) was launched in October 1997 at the Second Summit of Heads of State and Government of the Council of Europe. It aims at protecting human rights, promoting a human rights culture and consolidating democracy.

EDC is a series of practices and activities aiming at a better training of young people and adults for a more active participation in democratic life. EDC is multidimensional and includes political, legal, cultural, social and economic dimensions as well as the European and global dimensions.

EDC training is realised directly, through civic education and also through practices stimulating social participation. It is a part of formal and non-formal education. The project has to answer three main questions: what are the necessary values and competencies for a sophisticated European citizen; how to cultivate these values and competencies; and how to convey these values and competencies to others. The project activities were organised around four complementary axes: a reflection on the concept of EDC, sites of citizenship, education and support system, communication and dissemination.

Sites of citizenship are a series of practices in areas illustrating the current meaning of citizenship. Sites are an innovatory form of managing democratic life with regard to civil society, applying citizenship in schools, youth and cultural centres, regions or NGOs.

The Moldovan site of citizenship is based on the development of university democracy. The primary site's objective is the development of the capacity of students and young teachers to participate actively in the life of the institution and the community, to analyse and solve common problems and to prepare a team of trainers in the field of education for citizenship.

To make the university an active agent of the twenty-first century requires relatively new knowledge, competencies and attitudes. The first edition of the present document was issued in 2001 in order that today's students know and practise the rights and responsibilities of young citizens. The increased interest of young people in this document, as well as the need to introduce some modifications according to the new provisions of the legislation of the Republic of Moldova led to the elaboration of the second edition of the student charter.

We would like to emphasise our effective and fruitful collaboration with the Council of Europe, which has always supported our efforts and hopes.

The Work Team

Preamble

We, students of the Ion Creangă State Pedagogical University, members of the Students' League of the Ion Creangă S.P.U., trade-union organisations and other NGOs,

Making our starting point the secular aspirations of young people to study at a higher education institution taking advantage of certain rights and facilities expressed through free opinion and choice,

Taking into account that any higher education institution needs a document where student rights and obligations are outlined,

Striving for protection and promotion of students' interests,

Considering that it might improve the behaviour, and increase the level of interest and responsibility of the students towards their rights and responsibilities,

Being aware of our responsibilities, obligations and earnestness elaborating this Charter,

Reasserting the will to live in peace and concord in a country with equal rights for all its citizens,

Keeping in mind the irreversible processes of democratisation and assertion of freedom in higher education taking place in Europe,

Set Up the Students' Charter and declare it the Supreme Law of the students of the Ion Creangă State Pedagogical University in Chişinău.

PART I

CHAPTER I

Education – A national priority

Article 1 – Juridical basis

Students' rights and obligations are determined by the Constitution and legislation of the Republic of Moldova, reflected in the present Charter.

Article 2 – Right to education

Higher education is equally accessible to everyone according to their merits, regardless of nationality, gender, race, age, social origin and state, political and religious affiliation or penal antecedents.

$$(5,1,6.1)^{102}$$

Article 3 – Students' status

According to the legislation of the Republic of Moldova a person is considered to be a student from the moment the admissions board has made the final decision on enrolment.

(4, II, 2.1; 1,V, 5.6)

Article 4 – Students' right to know their rights and obligations

1. Each student has the right to recognition of his/her personality.

(6, 23.1)

2. Each student has the right to know his/her rights and obligations. For this purpose, the Student Charter is public and accessible to everyone.

(6, 23.2)

Article 5 – Equal rights

1. All students are equal in their rights and freedoms, regardless of race, nationality, ethnic origin, language, religion, gender, opinion, and political allegiance.

(6, 16.2)

2. For the purpose of social unity, the student's national culture and religious confession are respected.

(6,19.1)

---

[102] The references in parenthesis refer to the documents listed at the end of the Charter. The first digit refers to the number of the documents in this list, whereas the following digits refer to specific parts of the document in question.

Article 6 – Foreign students

1. Foreign students who study in higher education institutions of the Republic of Moldova have the same rights, freedoms and privileges as the students who are citizens of the Republic of Moldova.

(5, VI, 65.4)

2. Foreign students who study in the Republic of Moldova must comply with the country's legislation and respect its language, history, customs and traditions.

Article 7 – Language of study

1. According to the Constitution and Articles 18,19, and 20 of the Law on the Functioning of Languages on the Territory of the Republic of Moldova, the state provides citizens with the right to choose the language of education and training at all levels of education.

(5, I, 8.1; 1, I, 5.4)

2. Administrative authorities of the higher education institutions are obliged to respect the student's option and choice concerning the language of study at the respective institution based on the application form attached to the personal record.

3. The citizens' right to education and training in the mother tongue is provided by the creation of a certain number of education programmes and groups as well as conditions for their functioning.

(5, I, 8.2)

4. The Romanian language and history are compulsory subjects for all students and in all higher education institutions regardless of department or qualification.

CHAPTER II

Students' rights and obligations

Article 8 – Guarantee and protection of students' rights and interests

1. The state guarantees every student the right to an adequate living standard and to his/her physical, intellectual, spiritual and social development.

2. The state undertakes measures to provide assistance to students' education and development.

3. The respective competent authorities as higher education institutions, administrative, public, local and legal authorities ensure the protection of students' rights.

Article 9 – Protection of students from special categories

1. The state supports, partially or integrally, living costs during the study period of the students who need social assistance.

(5, IV, 57.4)

2. The state creates favourable conditions for endowed persons for studies in the country or abroad. This category of persons is established by a commission, appointed by respective ministers.

(5, IV, 57.6)

Article 10 – Freedom of expression, thought and conscience

1. Every student shall enjoy the freedom of thought, conscience, opinion, the freedom to reject any ideological barriers as well as the freedom of expression through any possible means.

2. The freedom of expression must not harm other persons' right to their own opinion or dignity.

(6, 32.1, 32.2)

Article 11 – Freedom of assembly

The student has the right to meet freely at the level of a group, course, University, etc.

(6, 40)

Article 12 – Right to information

1. Means of information are not subject to censorship.

2. Means of information are obliged to inform all students correctly, truly and fairly.

3. The student has the right to be informed truly by official sources about the decisions and stipulations linked to the organisation of the University's life.

(5, I, 4. A)

Article 13 – Access to justice

1. In case of violation of the rights and/or freedoms stipulated in this Charter, students have the right to appeal to a superior instance within the framework of the University or law bodies in order to satisfy those rights and/or freedoms.

2. No University instances can restrict the enjoyment of the students' rights and freedoms stipulated by this Charter and the legislation of the Republic of Moldova.

(6, 20)

Article 14 – Right to petition

1. Students have the right to appeal to superior administrative instances of the University by handing in petitions addressed on behalf of the signatories only.

2. In case of a legal organisation petitions may be addressed exclusively on behalf of the staff it represents.

(6, 52)

Article 15 – Right to inviolability, to protection against physical and psychological violence

The state ensures the students' inviolability, protecting him/her from any form of exploitation, discrimination, physical and psychological violence, not allowing contemptuous and cruel behaviour, insults and mistreatment, and involvement in criminal acts.

(6, 25.1)

Article 16 – Right to protection of dignity and honour

Students have the right to protect his/her own dignity and honour. The violation of the students' honour and dignity is subject to punishment according to the Law in force.

Article 17– Right to development of intellectual abilities

1. The state provides all students with equal opportunities and conditions for assimilating cultural and education values.

2. The state supports the setting up of different state and public institutions that contribute to the development of the students' creative abilities.

3. The state ensures access to the institutions named in paragraph 2 of the present article.

4. In conformity with the legislation in force the state supports the publication of newspapers, magazines and books for students.

(5, VI, 6.2)

Article 18 – Right to work

1. Each student has the right to have a paid job, according to his/her possibilities, health and professional training, and to be remunerated according to the Work Legislation.

2. The state protects students against economic exploitation and against work dangerous for their health, or that is an obstacle in their professional training, or that harms their physical, intellectual, spiritual and social development.

(5, I,11)

Article 19 – Right to work for students who have graduated from higher education institutions abroad

Citizens of the Republic of Moldova who have graduated from higher education institutions abroad have the right to take a job equal to those who graduated from similar institutions in the Republic of Moldova.

(5, V, 64.3)

Article 20 – Right to scholarship

1. A scholarship is a monthly allowance that is given each semester, with the exception of the summer vacation, to students whose studies are financed by the budget. Scholarships are established proportionally to the year of study and qualification.

(12, 1.1)

2. Students who have passed the exams during the examination period and demonstrated remarkable academic performance have the right to a scholarship.

(12, 2.1)

3. Students who transfer from an institution to another have the right to a scholarship according to the results of the following examination period as well as of the graduation examinations.

(12, 2.8, par. 1)

4. Students who transfer from one faculty to another within the framework of the same higher education institution have the right to a scholarship in conformity with the legislation in force.

(12, 2.8, par. 2)

5. In case of temporary loss of the capacity to work and which is confirmed by a certificate given by a medical institution a student who has a scholarship continues to receive the scholarship during his/her sick leave.

(12, 2.7)

6. Citizens of other states, who study in the Republic of Moldova, have a scholarship in conformity with stipulations of the protocol on bilateral collaboration.

(12, 6.2)

Article 21 – Types of scholarship

Students may have the following types of scholarship:

a. A social scholarship is awarded monthly, for each semester, to students from disfavoured families depending on the parents' annual income;

(12, 1.4, 4.1, 4.3)

b. A senate scholarship represents a monthly allowance that is given each semester to students showing remarkable academic performance (the average of the marks obtained during the previous examination period should not be lower than 8,5 in technical and agrarian qualifications, medicine, economics, mathematics, computer science, physics, chemistry, biology, and 9 in other qualifications), exemplary behaviour and active participation in the social life of the higher education institution;

(12, 1.7)

c. A nominal merit scholarship represents a monthly allowance that is awarded by the higher education institution to students who have displayed remarkable academic performance, exemplary behaviour and active participation in scientific research activities, conferences, workshops and competitions;

(12, 3.2, 3.3, 3.4)

d. Students may benefit from a scholarship awarded by economic agencies that wish to train qualified specialists with university degrees;

(12, 5.4)

e. Graduates of the higher education institutions with pedagogical specialisation have the right to a scholarship the size of which exceeds the size of the average scholarship by 40 per cent.

(18, 2)

Article 22 – Cases when students can be deprived of scholarship

1. Students at diverse public organisations, with the exception of sporting organisations, do not benefit from scholarships offered from the budgetary sources of the higher education institution.

(12, 2.4)

2. Students who are on academic vacation do not receive a scholarship after passing the examinations.

(12, 2.6)

3. Scholarship can be withdrawn, temporarily or for a semester, according to the Rector's order if the student commits offences or violates stipulations of the activity regulations and the statute of the higher education institution.

(12, 1.6)

4. Students exempt from fees cannot receive a scholarship.

(10, 6)

Article 23 – Right to rest

1. Every student has the right to rest and leisure.

2. Every student has the right to take part in different entertainment activities. He/she can also participate in the organisation of cultural and artistic life.

3. The state stimulates and supports the creation of a large network of extra-university institutions, sports buildings, stadiums, clubs, rest camps and other means for spending leisure time.

Article 24 – Right to assurance with medical service

Students have the right to be assured by the medical institutions of the Health Ministry with the whole complex of measures for their health protection.

(5, IV, 59)

Article 25 – Students' obligations

1. Every student is obliged to:

   a. respect the Legislation of the Republic of Moldova regarding education;

   b. respect the statute of the higher education institution at which he/she studies;

   c. respect the rights, interests and dignity of other students and teaching staff;

   d. respect and fulfil the curricula;

   e. abide by the organisational and administrative stipulations.

(1, IV, 4.18)

2. Students have other obligations mentioned in the regulation of the interior regulations of the educational institution.

(5, IV, 58.4)

Article 26 – Graduates' obligations

1. Graduates of the higher education institutions are obliged to demonstrate knowledge of the official state language in accordance with the curricula of the respective institution;

(5, IV, 58.2)

2. If a graduate who has studied on a contract base refuses to work or postpones the activity in the organisation or enterprise that recommended him/her for study for 5 years, he/she is obliged to compensate all study expenses.

(5, IV, 58.3)

CHAPTER III

Organisation of studies in higher education system

Article 27 – Admission to higher education institutions

1. Admission to higher education institutions takes place through examination and selection on the base of baccalaureate diplomas, high school certificates or equivalent acts of studies according to general criteria established by the Ministry of Education.

(5, II, 25.4)

2. Admission to universities is organised by the higher education institutions according to the general criteria established by the Ministry of Education.

(5, II, 27.3)

Article 28 – The organisation of higher education

1. A student can simultaneously study two specialties by undergoing admission exams; in this case he/she can benefit from a state scholarship during his/her studies for only one specialty.

(5, II, 25.6; 4, V, 5.1, 5.6, 5.7)

2. Graduates of higher education institutions can continue their education in a new field of specialisation at the same or another institution only after paying tuition fees that are registered and fixed by the Ministry of Education and the higher education institutions.

(4, V, 5.9; 5,1, 25.8)

3. Students also benefit from other rights stipulated and registered in the statute of the Higher Education Institution.

(5, IV, 57.3)

Article 29 – The organisation of studies in two fields of specialisation simultaneously

1. The student may study in parallel one other specialisation at the same higher education institution in which he/she studies his/her major.

(4,V, 5.1)

2. Parallel study may be undertaken by a student who has finished the first or second year with the average mark not lower than 9.00 (nine) in arts and economic sciences and no lower than 8.5 (eight point five) in natural and technical sciences.

(4, V, 5.2)

3. For parallel study both students whose study expenses are covered from the state budget and fee-paying students are eligible.

(4, V, 5.3)

4. Fee-paying students may study the second field of specialisation on the basis of a new contract. In this case, the fee for the second field of specialisation should be reduced with the sum that comes from the expenses for subjects that are stipulated by both education programmes.

(4, V, 5.4)

5. Students who study a programme with mandatory attendance can attend the second specialty simultaneously at either mandatory or free-attendance studies.

(4, V, 5.8)

6. According to the Regulations on organisation and development of the graduating examinations, if a person undertakes his/her study simultaneously in two fields and has not passed the university degree examination in his/her major, he/she has the right to retake it without the right to take the university degree examination in the second field of specialisation.

(4,V, 5.17)

Article 30 – Short-term studies

1. Students may study in reduced terms at any forms of education regardless of the financing methods.

(4, IV, 4.1)

2. Students may ask for reducing the term of study only after having completed the first two years or four sessions with marks not lower than 8 (eight).

(4, IV, 4.2)

Article 31 – Stages of taking exams (credit tests)

1. Students who do not pass the exams and the credit tests in two subjects have the right to take each exam or credit test once more. On the request of the teaching staff or of the student and with the Dean's approval, an examination board of three persons may be formed; the members of the teaching staff who taught the course in question are also included in this board.

2. If the student has not obtained passing marks after the second attempt, he/she may ask for permission to pass the exam again at the respective object.

3. In exceptional cases, at the student's request and with the agreement of the teaching staff, the Dean of the Department may approve the passing of some exams out of the planned session on the condition that the total number of examinations of the same specialty does not exceed three, according to the terms of this Article.

4. The Rector may allow a student to retake an examination for the purpose of improving his/her mark in no more than two subjects, in the same year of study, for students who have passed all exams of the respective year of study on condition that the marks obtained at the examination are not lower than 8 (eight).

(4, III, 3.8)

Article 32 – Absence at examinations

Students unable to take part in the examination session for good reason (illness, participation in republican and international contests or concerts) and whose absence is justified by required documents (medical certificate, decisions, orders, etc.) are permitted to take credit tests and examinations according to a special schedule. This schedule also includes students who:

    a. study according to a special, individual plan, approved by the department;

    b. have the right to study simultaneously in two fields of specialisation;

    c. take care of children under 3 years of age;

    d. take part in different curricular and extra-curricular activities (national or international seminars and conferences).

(4, III, 3.8)

Article 33 – Right to contest marks

The student may contest in written form the mark given by the examiner within 24 hours from the moment it was announced.

(4, III, 3.13)

Article 34 – Academic leave

Academic leave can be granted in case of loss of studying abilities in connection with chronic disease, surgical procedures, accidents, pregnancy and nursing a baby.

(4, VIII, 8.1)

Article 35 – Right to transfer

The student has the right to transfer from a higher education institution of another state to another similar institution in the Republic of Moldova and vice versa.

(4, IX, 9.10)

Article 36 – Rights of part-time students

1. Part-time education is one year longer than full-time education.

(5, II, 25.5)

2. Part-time students have the right to a supplementary vacation, keeping the average payment during the examination period – 40 days annually, if they have fulfilled the curricula.

(15, IV, 1)

3. For 10 months before the final examinations students have the right to a day off per week to prepare for their examinations, keeping 50 per cent of the payment or 1-2 days off per week, without keeping the payment according to the decision of the administration of enterprises, organisations, educational institutions where they work.

(15, IV, 3)

4. The administration of educational institutions, enterprises or organisations is obliged to offer part-time students an annual vacation during the examination period, laboratory work, workshops and examinations in educational institutions.

(15, IV, 4)

5. Part-time students cannot study in two fields of specialisation.

(15, IV, 8)

6. Students leaving their studies by their own decision can be re-established to study on the budget base, if there are vacancies; those who are expelled because of unsuccessful academic performance, abandoning of studies or because of other motives can be re-established only as fee-paying students.

(15, IV, 11)

CHAPTER IV

Graduation from higher education institutions and activity after graduation

Article 37 – Graduation from higher education institutions

1. University education ends with final examinations, tests of qualification and a project or a graduation research paper;

(5, II, 27.4)

2. Graduates who have passed final examinations successfully are awarded a university degree in the field of specialisation and a licensed diploma;

(5, II, 27.5)

3. Graduates of higher education institutions who studied in two fields of specialisation are conferred two diplomas.

(13, 1, par. 2)

4. Graduates of higher short-term education institutions who have passed their final examinations and have presented their graduation research papers are conferred a diploma of higher short-term education in the corresponding field of specialisation.

(13, 1, par. 3)

5. Foreign citizens who have passed the final exams are conferred a licensed diploma and an analytical programme.

(16, II, 2.10)

Article 38 – Graduation exams failure

1. Graduates who fail a graduation exam receive a certificate of graduation.

(16, II, 2.11)

2. Graduates who fail all the graduation exams receive a certificate of graduation. In this case, graduation exams can be taken at most twice during 3 years.

(5, II, 27.6)

3. Foreign citizens, who study in higher education institutions in the Republic of Moldova and who fail the graduation exams and do not receive a diploma, have the right to ask for a certificate, mentioning the qualification and the year of graduation.

(13, 11)

Article 39 – Acts of graduation

1. Graduates of higher education institutions receive concomitantly with graduation diploma or university degree diploma a Diploma Supplement, in conformity with the model elaborated by the European Commission, the Council of Europe and UNESCO/CEPES.

(11, 2)

2. If the graduation document is lost or if for any reason it is not valid, the education institution issues a duplicate of the respective act against payment. The Diploma Supplement is valid only when presented with the diploma.

Article 40 – Employment of graduates of state higher education institutions

1. Students who study on a budget base are obliged to work three years in unities to which they are assigned by the Distribution Commission.

(14, 2.1)

155

2. Ministries and state institutions that do not provide the graduates with a job according to conditions stipulated in the distribution certificate, are obliged to employ them in conformity with the legislation in force, covering all financial expenditures linked to the transfer of the graduates and their family members to a new place of work offering an allowance.

(14, 2.14)

Article 41 – Employment

1. In cases where the Distribution Commission cannot offer a job to a graduate, he/she has the right to find a job independently and for this purpose receives a special certificate.

(14, 2.6)

2. Graduates have the right to be employed independently if they:

a. cannot work in the field of their specialisation in conformity with Commission of Expertise of Work Capacity and Consultative Medical Commission;
b. have a parent/spouse with a handicap of I or II categories and who cannot be provided with a job where they live permanently (in the absence of other family members);
c. cannot be provided with a job where the spouse fulfils his/her military service.

(14, 2.7)

3. Graduates of private higher education institutions as well as those who study on a contract basis at state education institutions, all expenses being supported by physical and/or legal persons, are employed in conformity with contracts signed with physical and legal persons or independently.

(14, 3.1)

Article 42 – Obligations of young specialists

1. In case of resignation before the expiry of one year of activity, the young specialist is obliged to return the sum of allowance given by the institution.

(14, 2.10)

2. In case the young specialist refuses to come to the work place in conformity with the distribution or suspends his/her activity before the established three-year term has expired, he/she is obliged to return in the state budget all the expenses for their education as it has been calculated by the educational institution according to the norms established by the Ministry of Education and Ministry of Finances.

(14, 2.12)

Article 43 – Rights of young specialists in the field of education

1. Young specialists in their first years of teaching career have the right to a 10 per cent increase of the unique allowance and the salary rise.

(17, Annex 2, 1)

2. Young specialists have the right to be provided by the library with the teaching materials necessary to organise the educational process as well as to be subscribed to periodical issues on the local public administration authorities' account.

(17, Annex 1, 7)

3. Young specialists have the right to be provided with accommodation, electric energy and combustibles during the first three years of teaching.

(17, 4)

Article 44 – Specialised post-university education[103]

1. Graduates who have university degrees may continue their education at post-university courses organised at higher education institutions or at institutions of scientific research.

(5, II, 29.1)

2. A master's degree implies obtaining profound knowledge and practical skills in the most important fields of science in order to be employed or continue education for a doctoral degree.

3. Post-university education ends with the conferring of a diploma and the award of the Master's degree.

(5, II, 29.3)

CHAPTER V

Defence of students' rights

Article 45 – Participation in decision making

1. Every student has the right to active and responsible participation in University life.

(5, IV, 57,1.D)

2. The student has the right to represent individually or through delegated people the interest of a group, students' association, etc.

---

[103] In the Moldovan higher education system, this term is used for second cycle ("Master's") degrees.

Article 46 – Students' rights regarding trade-union organisation

As a member of a trade-union organisation every student has the right to:

a. elect and be elected in trade-union institutions;

(8, IV, 19.1)

b. take part in activities organised by trade unions;

(8, IV, 19.5)

c. benefit from free financial and legal assistance;

(8, IV, 19.6)

d. be protected by the trade union within state juridical and economic organisation;

(8, IV, n. 4)

e. benefit from moral and financial support;

(8, IV, 19.6)

f. be informed of the activities and decisions of the trade union;

(8, IV, 19.2)

g. have free access to documents (reports) at the expense of the trade union's budget;

(8, IV, 19.2)

h. make suggestions of more efficient ways of spending the budget;

(8, IV, 9.2)

i. benefit from the trade union's cultural and sport services, vacation and holiday centres;

(8, IV, 18.3)

j. benefit from the material and moral support on behalf of the trade union during the strike period in accordance with actual legislation;

(8, IV, 22.1)

l. make use of rights and advantages in accordance with the statutes that are established by the primary organisation;

(8, IV, 19.9)

m. resign his/her membership status of a trade-union organisation member, withdrawing the membership card application form.

(8, IV, 16)

Article 47 – Student duties regarding the trade-union institutions

As a member of a trade-union organisation the student has the obligation to:

a. respect the statute of the trade union;

(8, IV, 20.1)

b. participate actively in the implementation of the decisions adopted by trade-union institutions;

(8, IV, 20.2)

c. stop activities damaging to the trade-union movement;

(8, IV, 19.5)

d. participate in the activities of the trade-union institution;

e. pay the membership fee in accordance with the statute of the trade union and carry out thoroughly the membership duties within the trade union.

Article 48 – Sanctions

1. Violation of Internal Regulation of the higher education institution by the student leads to his/her sanctioning, and possibly to expulsion.

(5, IV, 58.5)

2. Corporal punishment and use of any forms of physical or psychical violence methods are forbidden in higher education institutions.

(5, IV, 57.1)

Article 49 – Presumption of innocence

In case a student is accused of violating University Regulations, he/she is considered innocent and is not punished until his/her guilt is proved.

(6, 21)

Article 50 – Right to self-defence

A student cannot be sanctioned without giving him/her the opportunity to motivate his/her actions.

Article 51 – Temporary sanctions

Regardless of the student's nationality, sex, age, ethnical origin, the sanctions are temporary and proportional to the committed offence.

Article 52 – Expulsion

The student can be expelled from the institution if he/she has committed serious and/or repeated offences.

(4, VI, 6.1)

Article 53 – Exemptions from sanctions

1. The student cannot be sanctioned if he/she has not fulfilled his/her obligations for health reasons or other circumstances beyond his/her control.

(9, 1)

2. The expelled student can repeat the academic year by paying the fee for the certain year of studies, regardless of the way of financing: on a budget or contract basis.

(4, VI, 6.5)

PART II

Place of living

CHAPTER I

Distribution of accommodation in student hostels

Article 54 – Right to live in student hostels

1. The right to live in a hostel belongs to students who are single or married, for the period of studies in the educational institution.

(3, I, 1, Annex 2)

2. When transferred to another institution, the student loses his/her right to live in the hostel of the institution he/she has left.

(3, II, 7, Annex 2)

Article 55 – Allocation

The student is given the right to live in a hostel by the trade union of the higher education institution, based on the recommendation given by the Dean's office. In accordance with the above stated decision, the order on the allocation of accommodation is issued by indicating the number of the room and the period of time for which it is given.

(3, II, 8, Annex 2)

Article 56 – The students' council of the hostel

1. A hostel tenants' council, consisting of a chair, deputy chair, floor monitors, and other persons in charge, is elected to implement the students' self-administration in the hostel and to organise cultural, sport and educational activities.

(3, III, 14, Annex 1)

2. The council's decisions are binding for all the tenants of the hostel.

(3, III, 15, Annex 1)

3. The council has the right to adopt the warning and punishing decisions stipulated by the present Hostel Order.

(3, III,16, Annex 1)

CHAPTER II

Tenants' rights and obligations

Article 57 – Rights of the tenant

The tenant has the right to:

a. use the space for socio-cultural life in the hostel, equipment and inventory, also to benefit from the communal services of the hostel;

b. ask for repair of or replacing the worn-out equipment, inventory, furniture, used linen and also for replacing the deficiencies mentioned above in the cultural-communal services;

c. elect the council of the hostel and to be elected as a member of this council, take part in the cultural and sport activities, take part in the discussions dealing with life in the hostels;

(3, III, 12, Annex 2)

d. use the information sources of the hostel.

(3, V, 19, Annex 1)

Article 58 – Obligations of the tenant

1. The tenant is obliged to:

a. leave the room of the hostel within three days after receiving the diploma and when going on summer vacations;

(3, I, 5, Annex 2)

b. respect strictly the rules of the hostel;

c. preserve the property, the green spaces and the cleanliness of the hostel;

d. keep the room clean and tidy;

e. keep in the store room things which are not used on a day-to-day basis;

f. use reasonably electric energy, water and gas;

g. pay on time the established rent for the hostel in accordance with the actual tariffs and terms of staying in the hostel;

h. pay for any damages caused;

i. respect the anti-arson security rules, the rules of electric and gas installations, not to install additional electric facilities and equipment without the official permission of the hostel authority, etc.;

j. when leaving the hostel and temporary leaving on vacation the tenant is obliged to inform the hostel administrator two days before the departure and give back the hostel property, being issued with a bill.

(3, III, 13, Annex 2)

2. It is forbidden for the hostel tenant to:

a. transfer from one hostel to another or from one room to another without the administrator's approval;

b. change inventory from one room to another without administrator's approval;

c. mend or repair the electricity network, connect additional lightening installations;

d. allow outside persons to remain in the hostel for the night;

e. smoke or consume strong drinks, toxic substances and drugs in rooms, to be inebriated;

f. use any place or a room in the hostel in order to gain profit.

(3, V, 21, Annex 1)

Article 59 – Stimulations

The student who lives in a hostel and is well disciplined, who contributes to the improvement of living conditions and educational activities, can benefit from the following stimulations:

a. is placed in a better room;

b. is provided with a room in a hostel for the next year.

(3, VI, 22, Annex 1)

Article 60 – Sanctions

1. A tenant breaching the hostel may be subject to the following punishments:

a. reprimand;

b. reprimand with a warning;

c. suspension of the right to live in the hostel in the current year;

d. suspension of the right to live in the hostel for the remainder of his/her studies;

(3, VI, 23, Annex 1)

2. In the case of a tenant disagreeing with the sanctions, he/she can appeal to the administration, trade union and/or faculty authorities of the institution within 15 days commencing the date of sanctioning.

(3, VI, 24, Annex 1)

Article 61 – Decision about stimulation and sanction

The decision about stimulation and sanction is taken by the hostel administration together with the trade union and taking into consideration the recommendations given by the student's council and dean's offices.

(3, VI, 24, Annex 1)

Article 62 – Necessary inventory

The student living in the hostel is given the necessary inventory according to the regulations.

(3, II, 9, Annex 2)

Article 63 – Hostel rent

1. The student pays the rent for the whole period of staying in the hostel according to the established regulations.

(3, II, 10, Annex 2)

2. The hostel rent for students at the pedagogical institutions will not exceed 20% of the real cost.

(17, Annex 1, 3)

PART III

Education of fee-paying students

CHAPTER I

Rights

Article 64 – Rights of fee-paying students

Fee-paying students have the right to:

1. be admitted to any state or private institution of the Republic of Moldova in accordance with the institution's regulations;

(2, 2)

2. be qualified in accordance with the demands, scientific and technical achievements and necessities of professional activities in the conditions of market relations;

(2, 8)

3. participate in creating necessary conditions for effective development of the teaching-learning process;

(1, 4.17)

4. receive back the tuition fee in case of expulsion for health reasons or in case of missing classes (excepting the expenditures already undertaken);

5. choose the type of education: full/part-time education.

(2, 3)

Article 65 – Possibility to enter into another type of contract

The fee-paying student has the possibility to enter into another type of contract at any stage of his/her studies.

Article 66 – Modification of contract

The student has the right to amend the contract by making a document which will be an integrated part of the contract.

(2, 14)

Article 67 – Paying the fee

Depending on his/her financial situation student has the right to pay the fee by instalments, i.e. twice a year, at the beginning of each semester.

(2, 7)

Article 68 – Individual contracts

In case the applicant has not been admitted to the University being financed from a state budget he/she has the right to enter into an individual contract after the examination.

(2, 11)

Article 69 – Transfer of students

Transfer from one type of education to another is acceptable within the institution of higher education to other faculties with related fields of specialisation.

(4, IX, 9.1)

Article 70 – Enrolment on a transfer basis

The student can be enrolled at state education institutions by means of a transfer, on a contract basis from private education institutions (from corporative institutions), in accordance with the Provision of the Government of the Republic of Moldova, No. 357 dated 14.08.1995 and conditions of the Regulations.

(4, IX, 9.9)

Article 71 – Repeating an academic year

The student has the right to repeat an academic year in case of unsuccessful academic performance.

(2, 15)

Article 72 – Exemption from fee

The fee-paying student has the right to be exempted from a fee respecting the conditions of the Decision of the Government of the Republic of Moldova, No. 125 dated 15.02.2001.

(10)

Article 73 – Issuing of the graduation document

The student has the right to receive the graduation document when graduating from the University or when being expelled.

CHAPTER II

Obligations

Article 74 – Obligations of the fee-paying student

Fee-paying students have the obligation to:

a. pay the fee before the beginning of each academic year on needs of studies and social security of the student;

(2, III, 3.1)

166

b. follow the disciplinary regulations established by the University;

(2, III, 3.1)

c. perform on time all the tasks concerning the curricula in a given field of specialisation;

(2, III, 3.3)

d. write the research and diploma project in the field of specialisation;

e. fulfil the conditions of the contract;

f. students have to reregister not less than three months prior to the expiry of their contract;[104]

g. cover the expenses in case productive or pedagogical practice is undertaken abroad;

h. enter into the contract with legal representatives (if the student is under 18).

(2, 12)

Article 75 – Amount of the fee

The amount of the fee required for giving qualification to a specialist is established in order not to exceed the expenditures done in the previous year.

(2, 4)

Article 76 – Fee for part-time studying

The fee for part-time studies cannot exceed 40% of the fee for full-time studies.

(2, 4)

---

[104] Contracts are established on a yearly basis and in most cases expire at the end of the study year.

The Student Charter is based on the following documents:

1. Regulations of the Ion Creangă State Pedagogical University, Chişinău, 2000.

2. Ministry of Education, Youth and Sport Order No. 240 of 9 April 1998: Regulations regarding the qualification of specialists at the state institutions of the Republic of Moldova, based on a contract including all expenses for study.

3. Decision of the Government of the Republic of Moldova, No. 125 of 15 February 2001: Rules for staying at students' hostels of higher education institutions in the Republic of Moldova.

4. Ministry of Education, Youth and Sport Order No. 47 of 24 April 1997: Regulations of organisation of the process of studies in higher education institutions in the Republic of Moldova.

5. The Law of Education of the Republic of Moldova, Chişinău, 1995.

6. The Constitution of the Republic of Moldova, Chişinău, 1994.

7. Youth Law, Chişinău, 1999,

8. Statute of Education and Science Trade Union in the Republic of Moldova, Chişinău, 2000.

9. The European Convention on Human Rights (ECHR) as amended by Protocol No. 11, Strasbourg, 1998.

10. Decision of the Government of the Republic of Moldova No. 125 of 15 February 2001 concerning regulations and provisions of the right to be exempted from the fee for studies of the students of state institutions of education enrolled on contract basis.

11. Order of the Ministry of Education of the Republic of Moldova No. 143 of 2 May 2002 concerning issuing of the Diploma Supplement.

12. Appendix to Order of Ministry of Education and Science of the Republic of Moldova No. 502 of 2 August 2000 about the endorsement and application of the regulation concerning the ways and conditions of offering scholarship to students from higher education institutions.

13. Instruction concerning the issuing, completing and keeping acts of studies at higher education institutions in the Republic of Moldova, endorsed by Decision No. 22/4 of 6 June 2000.

14.   Regulation concerning employment of graduates of state higher education institutions, endorsed by the Collegium's decisions of the Ministry of Education of the Republic of Moldova No. 4.4/8 of 1 November 2001.

15.   Regulation of the organisation of part-time higher education institutions, endorsed by the Collegium's decision of the Ministry of Education of the Republic of Moldova No. 3.4/3 of 27 September 2001.

16.   Regulation of the organisation and process of the graduating examination in higher education institutions, endorsed by decision of the Council of the Ministry of Education No. 24.4.1 of 19 March 1996.

17.   Decision of the Government of the Republic of Moldova No. 542 of 3 May 2002 concerning support of students from state higher education institutions with a pedagogic profile and young specialists active in the domain of education.

18.   Order of the Ministry of Education of the Republic of Moldova No. 542 of 11 June 2002 concerning the support of students from state higher education institutions with a pedagogic profile and young specialists active in the field of education.

List of contributors

Editor

Sjur Bergan is Head of the Council of Europe's Department of Higher Education and History Teaching and Secretary to its Steering Committee for Higher Education and Research. He is a frequent contributor to the debate on higher education policies in Europe, the author of many articles and editor of *The Heritage of European Universities* (with Nuria Sanz, 2002) and *Recognition Issues in the Bologna Process* (2003).

Authors

Angela Garabagiu is Administrator in the Council of Europe's Division for Citizenship and Human Rights Education. She has worked extensively on issues of education for democratic citizenship at intergovernmental level as well as with individual countries, in particular the countries of the Commonwealth of Independent States.

Sergiu Musteață is Associated Professor at the History and Ethnopedagogy Faculty of the Ion Creangă State Pedagogical University in Chişinău and is the Moldovan co-ordinator for the Council of Europe's project on Education for Democratic Citizenship. His research interests focus on Ancient and Early Middle Age Archaeology and History as well as Cultural Heritage and history school textbooks. He is President of the National Association of Young Historians of Moldova and a member of the Bureau of the Association of Historians of the Republic of Moldova.

Annika Persson works with the Swedish Ministry of Education and represents Sweden in the Bologna Follow-Up Group. In autumn 2002, she was seconded to the Higher Education Division of the Council of Europe.

Frank Plantan is Associate Director of the International Relations Program of the University of Pennsylvania and was Executive Secretary of the pilot project on the University as Site of Citizenship.

Sales agents for publications of the Council of Europe
Agents de vente des publications du Conseil de l'Europe

AUSTRALIA/AUSTRALIE
Hunter Publications, 58A, Gipps Street
AUS-3066 COLLINGWOOD, Victoria
Tel.: (61) 3 9417 5361
Fax: (61) 3 9419 7154
E-mail: Sales@hunter-pubs.com.au
http://www.hunter-pubs.com.au

BELGIUM/BELGIQUE
La Librairie européenne SA
50, avenue A. Jonnart
B-1200 BRUXELLES 20
Tel.: (32) 2 734 0281
Fax: (32) 2 735 0860
E-mail: info@libeurop.be
http://www.libeurop.be

Jean de Lannoy
202, avenue du Roi
B-1190 BRUXELLES
Tel.: (32) 2 538 4308
Fax: (32) 2 538 0841
E-mail: jean.de.lannoy@euronet.be
http://www.jean-de-lannoy.be

CANADA
Renouf Publishing Company Limited
5369 Chemin Canotek Road
CDN-OTTAWA, Ontario, K1J 9J3
Tel.: (1) 613 745 2665
Fax: (1) 613 745 7660
E-mail: order.dept@renoufbooks.com
http://www.renoufbooks.com

CZECH REP./RÉP. TCHÈQUE
Suweco Cz Dovoz Tisku Praha
Ceskomoravska 21
CZ-18021 PRAHA 9
Tel.: (420) 2 660 35 364
Fax: (420) 2 683 30 42
E-mail: import@suweco.cz

DENMARK/DANEMARK
GAD Direct
Fiolstaede 31-33
DK-1171 KOBENHAVN K
Tel.: (45) 33 13 72 33
Fax: (45) 33 12 54 94
E-mail: info@gaddirect.dk

FINLAND/FINLANDE
Akateeminen Kirjakauppa
Keskuskatu 1, PO Box 218
FIN-00381 HELSINKI
Tel.: (358) 9 121 41
Fax: (358) 9 121 4450
E-mail: akatilaus@stockmann.fi
http://www.akatilaus.akateeminen.com

GERMANY/ALLEMAGNE
AUSTRIA/AUTRICHE
UNO Verlag
Am Hofgarten 10
D-53113 BONN
Tel.: (49) 2 28 94 90 20
Fax: (49) 2 28 94 90 222
E-mail: bestellung@uno-verlag.de
http://www.uno-verlag.de

GREECE/GRÈCE
Librairie Kauffmann
Mavrokordatou 9
GR-ATHINAI 106 78
Tel.: (30) 1 38 29 283
Fax: (30) 1 38 33 967
E-mail: ord@otenet.gr

HUNGARY/HONGRIE
Euro Info Service
Hungexpo Europa Kozpont ter 1
H-1101 BUDAPEST
Tel.: (361) 264 8270
Fax: (361) 264 8271
E-mail: euroinfo@euroinfo.hu
http://www.euroinfo.hu

ITALY/ITALIE
Libreria Commissionaria Sansoni
Via Duca di Calabria 1/1, CP 552
I-50125 FIRENZE
Tel.: (39) 556 4831
Fax: (39) 556 41257
E-mail: licosa@licosa.com
http://www.licosa.com

NETHERLANDS/PAYS-BAS
De Lindeboom Internationale
Publikaties
PO Box 202, MA de Ruyterstraat 20 A
NL-7480 AE HAAKSBERGEN
Tel.: (31) 53 574 0004
Fax: (31) 53 572 9296
E-mail: lindeboo@worldonline.nl
http://home-1-orldonline.nl/~lindeboo/

NORWAY/NORVÈGE
Akademika, A/S Universitetsbokhandel
PO Box 84, Blindern
N-0314 OSLO
Tel.: (47) 22 85 30 30
Fax: (47) 23 12 24 20

POLAND/POLOGNE
Głowna Księgarnia Naukowa
im. B. Prusa
Krakowskie Przedmiescie 7
PL-00-068 WARSZAWA
Tel.: (48) 29 22 66
Fax: (48) 22 26 64 49
E-mail: inter@internews.com.pl
http://www.internews.com.pl

PORTUGAL
Livraria Portugal
Rua do Carmo, 70
P-1200 LISBOA
Tel.: (351) 13 47 49 82
Fax: (351) 13 47 02 64
E-mail: liv.portugal@mail.telepac.pt

SPAIN/ESPAGNE
Mundi-Prensa Libros SA
Castelló 37
E-28001 MADRID
Tel.: (34) 914 36 37 00
Fax: (34) 915 75 39 98
E-mail: libreria@mundiprensa.es
http://www.mundiprensa.com

SWITZERLAND/SUISSE
Adeco – Van Diermen
Chemin du Lacuez 41
CH-1807 BLONAY
Tel.: (41) 21 943 26 73
Fax: (41) 21 943 36 05
E-mail: info@adeco.org

UNITED KINGDOM/
ROYAUME-UNI
TSO (formerly HMSO)
51 Nine Elms Lane
GB-LONDON SW8 5DR
Tel.: (44) 207 873 8372
Fax: (44) 207 873 8200
E-mail: customer.services@theso.co.uk
http://www.the-stationery-office.co.uk
http://www.itsofficial.net

UNITED STATES and CANADA/
ÉTATS-UNIS et CANADA
Manhattan Publishing Company
468 Albany Post Road, PO Box 850
CROTON-ON-HUDSON,
NY 10520, USA
Tel.: (1) 914 271 5194
Fax: (1) 914 271 5856
E-mail: Info@manhattanpublishing.com
http://www.manhattanpublishing.com

_____

FRANCE
La Documentation française
(Diffusion/Vente France entière)
124 rue H. Barbusse
93308 Aubervilliers Cedex
Tel.: (33) 01 40 15 70 00
Fax: (33) 01 40 15 68 00
E-mail: vel@ladocfrancaise.gouv.fr
http://www.ladocfrancaise.gouv.fr

Librairie Kléber (Vente Strasbourg)
Palais de l'Europe
F-67075 Strasbourg Cedex
Fax: (33) 03 88 52 91 21
E-mail: librairie.kleber@coe.int

Council of Europe Publishing/Editions du Conseil de l'Europe
F-67075 Strasbourg Cedex
Tel.: (33) 03 88 41 25 81 – Fax: (33) 03 88 41 39 10 – E-mail: publishing@coe.int – Website: http://book.coe.int